THE VOICE IN MY HEAD IS AN ASSHOLE

HOW TO TAME YOUR INNER CRITIC

DARRYL BLAKE

D1484536

To my daughter, the talented and beautiful Lily, who makes me want to be a better person (and less of an asshole) everyday . . .

Copyright © 2022 by Darryl Blake

All rights reserved.

No part of this book may be reproduced in any form or by any electronic or mechanical means, including information storage and retrieval systems, without written permission from the author, except for the use of brief quotations in a book review.

Although the publisher and the author have made every effort to ensure that the information in this book was correct at press time and while this publication is designed to provide accurate information in regard to the subject matter covered, the publisher and the author assume no responsibility for errors, inaccuracies, omissions, or any other inconsistencies herein and hereby disclaim any liability to any party for any loss, damage, or disruption caused by errors or omissions, whether such errors or omissions result from negligence, accident, or any other cause.

This publication is meant as a source of valuable information for the reader, however it is not meant as a substitute for direct expert assistance. The content of this book is for informational purposes only and is not intended to diagnose, treat, cure, or prevent any condition or disease. You understand that this book is not intended as a substitute for consultation with a licensed practitioner. Please consult with your own physician or healthcare specialist regarding the suggestions and recommendations made in this book. The use of this book implies your acceptance of this disclaimer.

CONTENTS

CONTENT WARNING

This book contains references to self-harm, suicide, depression, anxiety, and other mental health conditions.

A special note to anyone who might be suffering depression, anxiety, or any other mental health challenge. These are real, physical conditions. Please don't try to go it alone. Make sure you are getting help, ideally from a mental health professional. While the information in this book can be a useful resource, it may be extremely difficult to incorporate the concepts on your own, because the condition itself may interfere with your ability to think, feel, and act clearly. If in doubt, please talk to someone. You are not alone.

PART I

UNDERSTANDING THE INNER ASSHOLE

1

A MUTINY OF ASSHOLES

April 14, 1982

Seventy days lost at sea.

An epic story of survival.

The crew begs and moans pitifully, "We can't go on. We need more water." Barely recognizable, they lay on the decks burned beyond recognition, scarred and shriveled versions of their former selves. They suffer under soul-scorching sun for over seventy days at sea, shipwrecked and lost to the world. Fresh blisters bubble up between layers of earlier burns and abrasions that refuse to heal. Nothing, including skin, has a chance to dry out. Salt, literally rubbing into every wound in a never-ending cycle of soul-destroying wind and waves.

Meanwhile, the decaying rubber life raft taunts them with its written guarantee to stay afloat for forty days. Small comfort as they approach two months lost at sea, holding their raft together with improvised lashings and plugs of whatever can be scavenged to patch holes and tears. Keeping themselves afloat through constant use of the hand pump in a never-ending battle with the punctured, deflating tubes.

The captain has lost a full third of his body weight—hunger and thirst his constant companions. His tongue has swollen, pressing against the inside of his mouth, and making it painful to speak.

"No, we can't have more water. We've used our ration for the day. We need to save our supplies, or we'll never make it to landfall."

"But we'll never make it if we don't get water. We can't last much longer like this, we're dying," replies the crew. Indeed, already assumed dead by authorities, no one is searching for them. No one is expecting them to survive being lost at sea for this length of time. They are on their own, abandoned, as the argument rages on.

"We've done all we can. Let us have the water."

"No, we need to save it until we really need it."

"But we can't go on without it."

Like the surrounding ocean, the argument stretches on with no end in sight. The captain wants to agree with the crew, give in, and greedily consume the rest of the water in one last hurrah. Surely that's better than this agonizing "drip feed," the measly ration that never comes close to satisfying their aching thirst. But he knows their only chance of rescue is to make the water last. To stay afloat long enough for their decaying life raft to drift its way into the busy shipping lanes they have been limping towards over the previous two months.

How many times has it come down to this? Survival depending on who wins the battle of words. Will it be the captain as he reasons and resists in equal measure, rallying the voices of dissent with stories of hope? Stories of passing ships or landfall if they can make it just another day, perhaps tomorrow, always tomorrow.

Or will it be the crew? The long-suffering crew, the voices of despair and disappointment. Each day bringing fresh disasters both large and small. Another hole in the raft, another battle with sharks, another ship that sails right past without noticing them. Will their voices win out? Will they abandon the effort, giving in to the ever-present anxiety and depression that lurks in the shadowy depths below? Everything rides on this simple choice. A choice that must be remade constantly, as each new challenge throws fresh salt in their wounds. It would be so easy to give up, to lie down, to sleep, and forget. To stop fighting this battle and let the waves roll over them.

———————

THE CAPTAIN who inspired this story is Steven Callahan*. A whale or giant shark sank Steve's boat during a solo crossing of the Atlantic in 1982. But wait a minute, a solo crossing? Didn't I just describe the ongoing battle between Captain Steve and his crew? Yes. The events that inspired the story above happened - with one exception. Steven Callahan was alone when his boat sank, spending the next seventy-six days fighting for his survival in a small, slowly disintegrating rubber life raft. He had arguments with the crew. Just not a real, physical crew. The arguments in his daily fight for survival were all in his head, between the voice he referred to as the captain and other parts of himself that he identified as the long-suffering crew.

The voices he referred to as the crew wanted to give up, surrender to fate, and slip away from all the pain and suffering. To drink all the water and eat all the food. Meanwhile, the captain was the voice within that refused to forget about tomorrow, believing from deep within his soul that victory was possible, that his family was waiting for him, that he could make it. If he stuck to his plan and focused on his goals, tomorrow would be better. And if not, then maybe the next day, or the next. This part of him that focused on hope, not fear, was determined to see him through his challenges.

It is a battle we've all faced. The challenge of choosing hope over fear. Action over distraction. The challenge of moving beyond guilt that binds us to the past and anxiety that torments us with an unknown future. Like Captain Steve, the real battles of our lives are the ones that scratch and claw their way up from within. These are the real enemies, the disowned aspects of the self, the voices of bad habits and disabling beliefs, our fears and our regrets.

The ultimate truth—one each of us must face—is that nobody "out there" can fix our lives for us. Nobody can save us from ourselves. Only *we* can face the inner battles that rage daily between the inner assholes in our heads. The demons that are forever circling just below the surface like sharks beneath the captain's raft, ready to grab and pull us under. The voices that start out small but would swallow us whole if we were to let them.

Can we beat these inner voices of anxiety, fear, and regret that pop up like an insane, never-ending game of whack-a-mole? The voices of lost arguments, insults still felt, and regrets that still hurt. Of parents that bruised, bullies that tormented. Voices that wouldn't die, taking up residence in our heads as if tattooed on our brains.

Can we do better than let the perverse comfort of well-worn patterns justify our habits of avoidance as we stream the latest Netflix series? Are we able to stop numbing ourselves through our addiction to food, social media, and online shopping? Addictions to stories that others construct for us, but *we* end up living. Sure, they may not be working for us anymore, but we do them so well it's hard to give them up.

Our challenge is no different from that faced by Captain Steve. For Captain Steve's ultimate challenge, the one that would determine his success and his very survival is also ours. It is the challenge of overcoming our negative voices and the dark passengers within. The challenge of living our unled life, the life we carry within us as a possibility. The life that is constantly at risk of falling prey to the sharks of the mind and circling voices telling us we are not enough. Not deserving of happiness, of love, or freedom from fear. Voices reminding us of our limitations, our shortcomings. Either we tackle these voices or succumb to them. This is our choice. Captain Steve's epic story of survival reminds us that success over these voices is possible. It is possible to choose which voices we nurture, and which voices we listen to.

This book is a guide to overcoming the inner voices that drag us down. In Part 1, we'll come to understand our inner voices, using the latest evidence-based research as a guide. In Part 2, we'll develop a range of practical tools and approaches for living a life free of the tyranny of the inner asshole. Some ideas are simple and can be implemented straight away. Some take practice. And others are significant interventions that require considerable thought and planning. All can help. Most require some effort and practice, while some are almost too simple to believe.

And any one of the ideas, tools, and strategies can be the one
that changes everything.

-----

*FOR A GREAT READ, I recommend Steve's book, *Adrift: Seventy-
Six Days Lost at Sea.*

2

ORIGIN OF A SPECIES... EVOLUTION OF THE ASSHOLE

Circa 50,000BC

Barry and Forrest Flintrock move quietly and purposefully through the lush grasslands of the East African savanna. The path is one they have used most days over the last month. They walk at a relaxed pace as the morning sun breaks through the steamy mist of dawn, heading towards the fresh blue waters of the lake.

Then Forrest stops. He's heard something in the bushes just off to his left. A slow crunching of grass stalks as they break underfoot, and a low growling noise like a deep purr. The purr kitty makes, but only if she weighs in at 300 pounds. Forrest's heart stops dead, then seemingly at the same time starts racing at an impossible speed, feeling like it is going to jump out of his chest. A lion, or maybe a tiger, is stalking them, tracking their progress just through the screen of grass as they move along the path. He doesn't make a noise, but he hears a voice inside his head screaming at him, *f*#k, f*#k, f*#k, do something. Run! Now!*

And he does. Faster than he's ever run before. All the way back to the camp where his family and friends are, providing the relative safety of numbers, shelter, and weapons. Meantime Barry, who'd been oblivious to the rustling in the grass, was being torn to bloody shreds by not one but two large, fully mature lions. The lions had been lying in wait on the path all morning, waiting for someone or something to come heading down toward the watering hole.

Antelope, warthogs, and an assortment of other animals, both large and small, often used the track. But this has been a bonus catch for the lions. To have a large, juicy, and relatively defenseless creature like Barry stumble into their ambush. One that can't fight back or make them exert enormous amounts of energy in a chase for miles across endless plains. And Barry would provide enough food to keep them full for two or three days to come. Yes, life must have seemed pretty sweet at that moment for the two lions as they tore into Barry's still living body, fighting to get to the steaming organs in his shredded torso, as Barry's high-pitched screams drifted across the valley floor. Sucks to be Barry . . .

The events described above occurred 50,000 years ago. Approximately. Oh, and Barry and Forrest Flintlock were not their real names—at least I don't think so. But you can bet the scene described occurred many times during the history of early humans as they did their hunter-gatherer thing on the plains of East Africa. Someone eaten by a lion, others getting away. So, let's think about the ones that got away. The ones that lived to tell the tale. To live another day and ultimately mate with someone else, passing on their genetic material and contributing to the gene pool you and I share today.

Forrest is one of those lucky ones, and we pick up his story just a few weeks later, back out on the trail doing a little more hunting and gathering. Let's say Forrest hears what sounds like the pitter-patter of gigantic paws in the grass to his left. Again, with the man-eating wildlife. His inner voice knows about this. His brain immediately screams at him, *Lion! F*#king Lion!! Run!!* Or something to that effect. And off he goes, breaking the land speed record for prehistoric man as he races back to camp.

Meantime Jerry, his companion on this expedition, also hears the noises coming from the nearby grass. But Jerry is renowned throughout the tribe as being a bit of a "hippie-type," always seeing the best in situations. You know, that glass-half-full type of hairy little prehistoric man. As the eternal optimist, Jerry pauses, and rather than panicking, he lets his natural curiosity drive his behavior as he cautiously approaches the edge of the grassy trail. He wonders if there really is something in the bushes . . . perhaps if he is lucky, a delicious rabbit or chewy but nutritious little jungle fowl. Mmm, he thinks, *I feel like chicken tonight . . .* That was the last thing Jerry's inner voice would ever say to him.

Suddenly, the same lion that had eaten Barry a few weeks earlier, launches itself from behind some bushes, the impact knocking Jerry to the ground. Immediately clamping its jaws around Jerry's head, it crushes down with enough force to smash the bones of his skull before he can even scream in terror. No more Jerry genes to pass on to the next generation. Less glass-half-full genes, and more of the run-Forrest-run genes getting shared around.

Fast forward another few weeks, and by now, Forrest is getting jumpy about the whole going-for-a-walk-along-the-path type of scenario. He is worrying a lot about getting eaten, even when he's not out hunting. He's questioning his life choices constantly . . . *maybe I should have been an accountant rather than a hunter . . . ?* His inner voice is in a continuous battle with itself over what to do when he's out hunting. Where should he place himself? Should he walk at the front of the pack or somewhere in the middle? Should he just call in sick for work tomorrow and hang back with the gatherers? Is it all worth the risk? Where does the path end? What is this thing called life, anyway? Okay, maybe that last part is a bit deep for our hairy little ancestor, but you see where I'm going with this.

Forrest's inner voice has been growing into an inner asshole. One that's keeping him awake at night, worrying about stuff. All types of stuff. Picking through the bones of what's gone wrong or what could go wrong. Doubting his ability to get it right. Yet, this type of thinking has saved his life. It's been a helpful attribute. It confers what are known as adaptive advantages to Forrest and those like him, the worriers, the anxious and the hypervigilant. Because in the frightening shit-show of living bare-assed-naked in a jungle full of things that want to eat you, being hyper-sensitive to movement in the bushes and thinking the worst of what might happen can be a positive adaptation. It can keep you alive because anything that frightens you will probably kill you.

Living a modern life with a prehistoric mindset

Our problem as modern humans is that millions of years of natural selection have taken place in a perfect environment for shaping our minds to look for the worst. To be fearful or worry, run away, or get angry fast—fright, flight, or fight. This has led to a bias toward what science would call false positives when assessing the level of danger around us.

A false positive is when we wrongly think a particular situation or condition is present. For instance, assuming there's a lion in the bushes is a false positive for lions when it's just the wind. A dangerous environment can favor these false positives because the alternative, a false negative such as assuming no lion, can get you eaten. It's better to be wrong a hundred times by panicking and running back to camp, but living to see another day, than to be wrong once by assuming there is no lion in the bushes and getting eaten. It makes sense to favor a bias toward false positives, given the risks and rewards involved.

Anyone with a more relaxed attitude about potential dangers simply didn't make it. They might have been right 99% of the time. No lion, just wind blowing the bushes. But it only took one error, one false negative, to be eliminated from the dating pool. This one mistake got them literally torn to shreds.

People ended up becoming attuned to the worst possible outcomes because it kept them alive, with free-floating anxiety becoming hard-wired into the species through generations of living in this type of environment. Eventually, all the owners of easy-going, laid-back, and positive inner voices were eaten. Why? Because they never jumped and were never suspicious, anxious, or prone to worry about the dangers that could have killed them. Their inner voices weren't constantly on their backs winding them up, reminding them how much they were at risk, what they had to lose, and how dangerous the world around them really was.

Ultimately, the people left standing were those that always assumed the unknown was dangerous, and that they always had to be on the defensive. The ones that reminded themselves, it's a scary, uncertain world, and I'm going to make sure I don't fall victim to anyone or anything. The ones with inner voices that became inner assholes.

In today's psychological parlance, the inner asshole, convinced by the experience of thousands of years of prehistoric dangers, has become hypervigilant and hypersensitive. Always on the lookout for danger and sensitive to the tiniest of "threats." Seeing challenges that just aren't there anymore. Getting angry at "that look" someone gives you. Hearing a put-down in every comment. Sensing a challenge in every gesture. And feeling mortal danger in every credit card bill.

In the meantime, the nature of the risks we face within our environment has changed far too rapidly for the scared inner asshole to adapt. The dangers around us were once fatal. The inner asshole got used to seeing its friends dying of hunger, being speared, or torn apart by wild beasts. But the threats of the modern environment, the things that make you pissed, are no longer the same. The driver that won't let you merge. The barista that took too long to make your chai latte. These things we get worked up about are no longer fatal. They won't leave us on the footpath, with our intestines shredded and our faces torn off.

These days, the threats that trigger the inner asshole to protect us don't need a fight, flight, or freeze response. Quite the opposite, they require us to remain calm, take a deep breath and consider the bigger picture. To use our imagination, tap into our inner strength—not our inner asshole. Where most threats in the past could either be run from or speared, neither solution works well when confronted by your boss asking why you were late to work. Try explaining either to HR.

Much of the inner dialog we'll explore in upcoming chapters is driven by this overblown and outdated fear response learned over thousands of years. Today, it may not be hungry lions driving our anxiety. But our inner asshole's fear response isn't that discerning. Its overreaction is just as crippling whether in anticipation of a lion in the bushes or the nagging fear of never being enough.

As we progress, we'll learn to talk our inner asshole back down off the ledge and rewrite our inner story for a healthier, happier life.

3

I HEAR DEAD PEOPLE

O k, that chapter heading was just to get your attention. Or was it . . . ?

In a way, I do hear dead people. I can still sometimes hear my deceased mother's voice in her native French, yelling "Basta!" at me when I was misbehaving as a child. She would shout and then get even angrier when I ignored her. When she was angry, she always seemed to forget that I didn't speak French. Which only made her madder because I had no idea what she was telling me to do. But to this day, certain things still trigger that voice in my head. A high-pitched string of crazy French talk, something about "ferme ta gueule!" and "petit merdeux!" I must look those up someday.

I'm sure it was something sweet . . .

We all hear the voices of other people, including those of the dead. Imagine, for instance, you're replaying in your mind Martin Luther King Jr. giving his well-known *I have a dream* speech. I'm betting that when you imagine him speaking, you hear it delivered in that famously rich baritone rhythm, not your own squirrely high-pitched whine. Or when you replay in your mind your partner's snippy comments made this morning during an argument, it's their voice you imagine. Not your own voice coming out of their mouth, right?

We sometimes carry around these voices of others for our entire lives. Echoes of our past. Dark passengers inspired by parents, schoolyard bullies, or relationships that turn bad. From unkind words to cruel taunts, comments that come back to haunt us in our hours of weakness.

And then there are the voices we generate ourselves.

Talking to ourselves

We all have our own inner dialog. You know the voice I mean. If you're not sure, it's the one that might be talking to you right now. Maybe it's saying something like, sure, I know what he means, or—hopefully not—what the hell is this guy talking about? Why'd I even pick this book? Who's he calling an asshole anyway . . .

Seriously though, it's completely normal to have a bunch of inner voices that seem to be constantly running through your head. It's also normal that these voices sometimes turn into dark forces—unwanted, intrusive, and out of control. But don't sweat it. They are simply a part of who you are and what it means to be human.

They serve a purpose, and we're going to learn how to put them back to work for us.

Why have an inner dialog?

Research on inner dialog points to its development from early childhood as a way of self-regulating thought and behavior.[1]

Essentially, we take over the voices of our parents or caregivers and begin to apply them internally. In this way, our mind provides a way to identify mistakes, advise how to do things "right," resolve problems and navigate successfully through the day.

Taking over the voices of our parents, stuffing a mini version of them inside our own minds for future reference, starts from an early age. We do this by mimicking the things we hear our parents say, gradually taking these instructions on as if they were our own.

For instance, as a child, we may be heard to quietly sub-vocalize the steps of a task previously taught by a parent. The process is learned and cemented as we repeat the steps or rules.

"First, take the lid off of the toothpaste."

"Then pick up the toothbrush . . . now go up and down (not across!) each tooth."

In doing this, we are creating patterns of behavior that will eventually become habitual and somewhat automatic. We are laying down rules that will drive us as adults. Voices that will speak up when we, or others, stray from those rules.

As adults, we do something similar when learning complex routines. For instance, we might repeat sub-vocally to ourselves a set of instructions given by a teacher or an instructor. A learner-driver might run through a mental checklist, telling themselves each step of pulling out from a stationary park. Ok, engage 'Drive,' keep my foot on the brake, release my park brake, check my mirrors, indicate, and so on.

This process will continue until the activity has become yet another unconscious pattern capable of guiding our future behavior. Creating a recording. An internal dialog ready to speak up when we or others need reminding of how things should be done. Perhaps, when mixed with a bit of impatience, appearing as the voice that screams at the driver in front to *use your f#@king turn signal idiot!* Or any other time our rules and procedures are broken by those around us.

Other research shows that our inner speech develops as a short-term memory strategy.[2] For instance, when repeating in our head a phone number until we can find a pen to write it down. It has also been linked to problem-solving, planning, and similar complex, conscious cognitive functions. In this way, our inner voice serves to assist working memory, keeping the thread of our reasoning, and applying our brain's logic component to process information and make decisions.

A simple example is when you use your inner voice as a kind of mental to-do list. For instance, upon waking, you might list in your head a reminder of the things you need to get done today. In these various ways, your inner voice helps you perceive and make decisions about the world, sorting and categorizing your thoughts, storing and recalling memories and their meanings.

When overused, however, this dialog turns into self-criticism. Intended to protect you from potentially dangerous behaviors and risky mistakes, it becomes controlling in its efforts to keep you safe. This is the dialog that thinks you exist to serve its fears and concerns, rather than the other way around.

In this way, the voice in your head becomes an asshole. And to make matters worse, there are hundreds of these inner voices running around the average person's head. Each with an opinion, lining up for a turn to tell you its problems, utterly oblivious to the other issues you have. Oblivious to how they're making you feel. More focused instead on rehashing the argument you had five years ago, with someone you don't talk to anymore, than allowing you to get back to sleep because you have work in the morning.

When our inner dialog turns into an asshole

The challenge of overactive inner voices has been with us for a long time. Around 2500 years ago, the Buddha described the actions of the human mind as being like that of a monkey, jumping wildly all over the place, without discipline or purpose. Random thoughts, problems, and anxieties popping out of nowhere, chattering and carrying on like a cage full of stirred-up chimps. Known in psychology as Automatic Negative Thoughts, or A.N.T.'s, these asshole thoughts become so intrusive that they seem to have a mind of their own, showing up out of nowhere and demanding our attention.

These psychological viruses become the back-seat driver of our feelings and moods. After a random minute of swirling thoughts about our credit card bill, we descend from carefree to anxious. Thoughts popping out of nowhere, starting with a mere whisper, and escalating to a roar, remaining stuck on play no matter how much we tell ourselves we've had enough.

Despite their hold on us, these voices and stories need not even make sense—often they are complete rubbish. You might be lying there wishing you could get to sleep, but your mind is busy trying to work out why glue doesn't stick to the inside of the container, or why penguins don't freeze. You know, the big questions in life . . .

Why do we get this nonstop dialog in our heads? Who are we talking to? Who is doing the talking? Have you ever stopped halfway through a running commentary in your head, and wondered just who you're providing the analysis to? And why you're explaining something you already know, back to yourself. I mean, which part of you thinks it needs to carefully instruct another part of yourself about that thing you should have said differently in an argument with a friend back in 2017?

Who is this helping? Who are you retelling the story to, and for what purpose are you telling it?

Let's look at where all this shit is coming from . . .

References

1. Alderson-Day, B., Fernyhough, C. (2015). Inner Speech: Development, Cognitive Functions, Phenomenology, and Neurobiology. Psychological bulletin, 141(5), 931–965.
2. Baddeley A., & Hitch G. (1974). Working memory In Bower G. H. (Ed.), Psychology of learning and motivation (pp. 47–89). New York, NY: Academic Press.

4

WHAT THE F@#K HAVE I BECOME?

The following is a dialog between a 3-year-old and a television interviewer on a cable channel. I have redacted all identifying features to protect the not so f@#king innocent . . .

Presenter: "Do you like [redacted ethnicity]?"

3-year-old: "No."

"Why don't you like them?"

"[Redacted ethnicity] are dogs and pigs."

"Who said this?"

"Our God."

"Where did he say this?"

"In the [name of the particular holy book redacted]."

The presenter responds approvingly:

"No parents could wish for [name of deity redacted] to give them a more believing girl than this . . . May [name of deity] bless her and her parents."

Nice kid . . .

But then, how could she know any better? If all she has ever been exposed to is hate-filled propaganda? Having grown up in a place where parents are urged by religious and political leaders to "nurse our children and grandchildren on hatred." Can she be expected to see such thoughts as evil? Or just plain ordinary, nothing more than a part of her background reality?

If you're a fish growing up in a sewer, can you even conceptualize how cloudy the water is, unless you land in a clean river one day?

Conditioned for failure

We are bombarded with messages from our parents, authority figures, and social environments since before the time we're born, with some research suggesting babies learn in utero from as early as the third trimester.[1]

Regardless of when exactly it begins, to be human is to be programmed by our early environment. As children, we are constantly being told what to believe and how to act. What is essential; right and wrong, good and bad. All these things— everything seen, heard, and felt—are recorded, at least temporarily, in our brain. Setting us up for a life we never had a choice over and a story we never had a say in. A story picked up from our caregivers' inner asshole and retold to us daily.

Messages repeated often or delivered with emotion, confidence, and certainty become wired into the childhood brain. These messages are programmed into the subconscious, waiting to be triggered in the future as the voice of our inner asshole. Perhaps you were told to "take a spoonful of concrete and harden the f@#k up" from the age of two every time something terrible happened? No problem. It probably explains why you're still telling yourself to tough it out or get yourself together as a 30-year-old. And still swallowing every negative emotion, wondering why you can't communicate your feelings to your family, friends and loved ones.

Taught to fear, hate, and worry

Maybe you were raised to believe that your neighbors are to be hated, feared, or loathed. Or to loathe yourself if you didn't live up to the expectations and standards of others. All absorbed unquestioningly by the infant brain. Because anything can seem normal when you're soaking in it. When you can't see what's outside the bubble . . . when you don't even know you're in a bubble.

Either consciously or subconsciously, we are programmed to react in fear and anger over things that make our parents or teachers angry and afraid. In this way, we end up carrying the reactions and paying the price for the hurts and prejudices of others, over issues that should never have been our stuff to deal with. As adults, these thoughts and feelings we grew up with become reflexive and automatic, with our negative inner asshole repeating them regularly, making sure we never forget.

There are these two young fish swimming along and they happen to meet an older fish swimming the other way, who nods at them and says, 'Morning, boys. How's the water?' And the two young fish swim on for a bit, and then eventually one of them looks over at the other and goes 'What the hell is water?'

David Foster Wallace

The trouble is that we have no way of field testing these instructions as young children. We can't identify which are good for us; harmful; or just pure evil.

Over the first few years of life, this programming fills our subconscious like filling up the drive on a computer. We become conditioned to believe all sorts of crap about ourselves. Maybe we are told we're too lazy, too stupid, too slow, or just not enough. You get the idea. Whatever it is, we absorb the messages around us like little sponges.

It's like one big f@#king circle of life, with each generation's shit passed on to the next. Hakuna-matata folks . . .

Programming that remains hidden in plain sight

We're usually left with no conscious memory of this potentially toxic mix of opinions, rules, and limiting beliefs we absorbed growing up. At age two, we had no idea that we were only receiving a skinny slice of reality. We couldn't know there were fishbowls with cleaner water we might have grown up in. Where we may have been raised to think of ourselves as angelfish rather than bottom feeders . . .

We end up with no point of reference as to why we feel so angry, sad, or afraid; why we flip out when people around us break specific rules, act in particular ways, or say certain things; or why we enforce certain habits on ourselves regardless of circumstance.

For instance, it may have never occurred to us—even though we're trying to lose weight—why we must finish everything on the plate. Is this helpful advice for someone trying to reach their weight goal? Or just a hangover from our great-grandparent's generation, slapped into our parents, and then told to us hundreds of times growing up? All based on a time during the 1930s Great Depression when every mouthful of food was desperately important to their survival. We're left navigating life in the 2020s carrying an inner voice guilting us for not eating everything on our plate. A voice that's nothing more than an echo of a rule that originated as a valid survival mechanism a century earlier.

We take our rules for granted, and end up frowning at the "strange" behaviors of others who didn't grow up at the receiving end of our conditioning. We then spend the rest of our lives trying to convince them they should act in specific ways, believe certain things, and live their lives according to certain principles and rules, just because we say so.

Meantime, we continue to judge ourselves by unexamined rules and expectations picked up from others, but now pushed down our throats by our inner asshole voices. We punish and diminish ourselves daily, reinforcing our own imaginary and borrowed limitations. We do this without ever realizing that we're just repeating someone else's opinions, fed to us when we were too young to know any better.

Sometimes these opinions have been internalized so strongly that they no longer even reach our awareness as dialog. Instead, they wash over us as unexplained feelings of sadness, separation, or anxiety. The words become a barely heard whisper, running a second story over whatever is happening around us. Fear writes this script, and the title is *I'll Never Be Enough*.

Fueled by these hidden fears and conditioning, each internalized story of the inner asshole lies in wait, ready to spew its agenda at every opportunity.

You are not the voices and stories in your head . . .

To understand your mind and the interplay of its many internal asshole voices, let's use the analogy of how a smartphone works. Your smartphone can be many things; a camera, a calendar, a weather forecaster, a messaging device and, well . . . even a phone. It depends on which application you choose to run. But one thing is irrefutable. The phone is not the apps.

Each of these apps has its own goals, rules, and ways of dealing with things. Individual apps don't care, unless programmed otherwise, if their goals conflict with other apps. On your phone, the map application doesn't know or care if it's screwing with the plans in your health app, by helping you find the quickest route to the store for some cigarettes. The apps are each doing a job, blindly adhering to their programming, without regard for the overall consequences of their activity.

The phone is something other, something much more significant than any of its apps. It is a sophisticated piece of equipment that can use the apps to "think" with. Yes, the apps are a part of the phone. But that's all they are. One part of a whole. And most important of all, we can reprogram the phone, deleting, upgrading, or replacing apps.

Like a smartphone is not its apps, you are not the voices in your head.

The voices are only one part of who you are and how your mind works. Just as a smartphone has many apps that run independently, each of your inner assholes operates autonomously, with its own goals and opinions. Independent of each other and often in conflict with your overall goals and peace of mind. Working to their own programmed scripts until they are turned off or until they reach their goal—just like an app on the phone.

For instance, once activated, the voice telling you to get ice cream will keep on nagging until you get the ice cream. Or until you distract the voice with a new goal. All these inner voices are just running like an app of the mind - they are not you.

For this reason, you should never make the mistake of identifying yourself with your current thoughts and inner voices. They are passing through your mind like clouds drifting across the sky. You may have been conditioned to hate or fear. You may have picked up the anxieties of your parents or society. But you are not these stories. You are the observer of these stories.

Next up, let's look at how these "apps of the mind"—our inner assholes—operate. To do this, we are going to explore "the many selves" model of the mind.

References

1. Marx, V., & Nagy, E. (2015). Fetal Behavioural Responses to Maternal Voice and Touch. PloS one, 10(6), e0129118. https://doi.org/10.1371/journal.pone.0129118

5

ASSHOLES HAVE A MIND OF THEIR OWN

Cyberdyne Systems 1997

The Skynet Funding Bill is passed. The system goes online August 4th, 1997. Human decisions are removed from strategic defense. Skynet begins to learn at a geometric rate. It becomes self-aware at 2:14 a.m. Eastern time, August 29th. In a panic, they try to pull the plug."

The Terminator, Terminator 2: Judgement Day

Like Skynet, our inner assholes have developed a mind of their own. They actively conspire to remove our mindful self from decision-making.

But what do they want?

• They want control.

• They have their own goals. They don't care about you as a person. They know what they want and won't stop until they get it.

• They collude with each other like a shadow government, often hidden from conscious awareness.

• When they appear, they are like a single-issue zealot, caring for nothing but their own agenda.

• They have a win-at-all-costs approach. They'd rather be right than happy, willing to burn the whole house down to make a point, to win the argument.

• Like any revolutionary seeking to overthrow the government, they know they must take charge of the media and control the narrative. To make sure you only get the news they want you to. For the inner asshole, that means throwing a filter over everything you see and hear, literally distorting your reality.

Do I sound like I'm exaggerating with these claims of insurgent assholes living inside your head? As bizarre as these claims may seem, I'm not making this stuff up. It's all based on well-established views in both psychology and neuroscience. Let's inspect the evidence for how our psyche operates. Full of inner assholes bossing you around, 24/7.

Understanding our "many selves"

As individuals, we share the sense that our behaviors result from conscious, deliberate choices. We assume a sense of control over our internal processes and decisions. We feel as if there is a central "I", a "self" in charge of our inner worlds. Yet, we also know that our inner worlds can be incredibly complex, full of conflicting desires, anxieties, and tensions. Various goals, good intentions, and desires jostle around like roommates in a crowded dorm.

Indeed, we often use the language of plurality, of "many selves" to explain our inner workings and dilemmas. We might discuss a relationship issue with a friend, explaining that "a part of me wants to stay with him, but another part of me realizes that it just isn't working out."

Exactly what are the parts we're talking about in this scenario? How many parts, personalities, or voices are in there, anyway? And just who is the "I" that we refer to so casually when thinking of ourselves?

"I am not one and simple, but complex and many."

Virginia Woolf, The Waves

Psychologists, religious scholars, and philosophers have pondered these questions for thousands of years. Just who are we? How and why do we think, feel, and act the way we do?

Carl Jung, recognized as one of the most influential psychiatrists of all time, talked about our mind being governed by thousands of what he referred to as autonomous complexes. Or what we are referring to as our inner voices. Circling just below the surface like the shark in Jaws, Jung described them as offering "resistance to . . . conscious intentions," coming and going as they please.

He said these complexes "lead a separate existence in the unconscious, being at all times ready to hinder or to reinforce . . . [our] . . . conscious intentions".[1] This explains so well the daily experience of many. Just think, for example, of the inner battle

assholes, and in the next chapter, we will single them out, identify and name them.

Doing this will help us manage our inner assholes and live our
best life, not our most familiar story.

References

1. Carl Jung (1955). Modern Man in Search of a Soul,
   Harcourt.
2. Huang, J.Y., Bargh, J.A. (2014). The Selfish Goal:
   autonomously operating motivational structures as the
   proximate cause of human judgment and behavior.
   Behav Brain Sci., 37(2), 121-35.
3. Michael S. Gazzaniga (2018). Consciousness Instinct,
   Farrar, Straus and Giroux.

6

WHAT'S IN A NAME...

You might wonder why it's essential, or even necessary, to identify and name your inner assholes. Why you should treat each one as if they are separate entities with their own histories, methods, and motives.

Naming the inner assholes allows you to see them for what they really are. They lose some of their power as you recognize *you are not the problem. They* are. *You* don't need "fixing;" you just need to stop listening to the ceaseless ravings of these lesser parts of yourself.

And this is where naming them comes in. By giving your inner voices names and identities, you create a clear separation between yourself and their relentless, destructive chatter. Once named, you can learn to identify them when activated; to understand their motives when they appear, and how to overcome them.

7

THE PREHISTORIC ASSHOLE

I magine taking a three-year-old child and telling them dozens of times a day for the next fifteen years of their life that they will be the best swimmer in the world.

You get them out of bed at 4am for an intensive workout consisting of six to twelve miles of swimming. Then it's off to the gym or track for weight training, sprints, yoga, and Pilates. Plus, a full day of schooling. Followed by an equally challenging afternoon session back in the pool. Welcome to a day in the life of an Olympics level swimming athlete.

Meantime, you fine tune their mind and body for the arduous process of competitive selection. Their body, tailored by fifteen years of preparation, becomes perfectly adapted to the task. To see off challengers at each progressive level of the sport as they climb the world rankings of professional swimmers. Winning race after race, becoming a contender for the record of fastest human on earth in the pool.

But things around them are changing. Global warming and water shortages across the planet lead to swimming being banned as a sport. Effective immediately, all swimmers are put onto baseball teams.

How do you think our swim champion would fare, thrown in at the deep end of this new sport, expected to compete against professionals in a completely different environment? I'm betting pretty poorly. They've never picked up a bat or ball in their life. They don't know the rules of the game. They can't hit and they can't catch.

They've had some of the best training in the world, but for the wrong sport. Yes, they are fit, intelligent and have a winning mindset. But they totally suck in their new environment . . .

Most of you reading this book face the same challenge as the athlete who prepares for swimming but suddenly gets thrown into baseball. Match-fit, but for the wrong game. Born into an environment that bears zero resemblance to the one that shaped your mind and body—through a million years of competitive selection—for success.

Our preparation as members of the human race has been for survival in places like the African savanna, the jungles of Borneo, or the prehistoric wetlands of Gondwana. We are the most recent in a long line of winners who outplayed, outwitted, and outlasted the hundreds of animals, famines, floods, storms, ice ages, volcanic eruptions, and diseases that wanted to kill us and our ancestors.

Hardwired into our genetic code is a blueprint for the physical and psychological attributes that made those ancestors winners in an unforgiving environment. But it's a lousy preparation for the game of life we have built since the development of agriculture, the industrial revolution, and the sudden move—as measured in evolutionary time-scales—from hunter-gathering into offices, factories, houses, and apartments.

Evolutionary change due to natural selection within a species is thought to take around a million years to stabilize. But the shift in our environment from hunter-gather to latte-sipping-hipster has "only" taken the last ten thousand years. The rules of the game have changed way too fast for our hardwiring to keep up. We've come armed with a stone-ax to a gunfight. Our Prehistoric Asshole, dressed in a loincloth and carrying a pointy stick for protection, is still there somewhere in the dark recesses of our minds. Trying desperately to deal with the modern world, using a template that stopped working the moment we traded tropical jungles for "urban" ones.

This template it uses contains 7 key themes for survival, driving the stories it whispers to us daily . . .

The 7 Stories of the Prehistoric Asshole.

1. Keep eating. Especially the fatty and sugary stuff!

For the last million years as hunter-gatherers, our ancestors would have spent most of their waking hours thinking about food; chasing, foraging, hunting, killing, and preparing it.

Life was fragile, living from meal to meal, often going hungry for days at a time. Our predecessors had to be super motivated to continue looking for food all the time if they were to survive. Hunger was simply our brain's hardwired signal to keep looking for food. Designed as an urgent and uncomfortable cue to make sure we paid attention, with research suggesting that hunger will reliably override our other drives and instincts.[1] No wonder we get "hangry". . .

We are powerfully driven to search out and eat whatever we can lay our hands on. Even in today's world of supermarkets, fast-food chains, and Uber Eats, every moment of hunger for the Prehistoric Asshole still feels like a critical emergency warranting urgent action. Once upon a time, this meant having to exercise for hours collecting berries or tracking wildlife. Now it means reaching for our phone and ordering in.

Essentially, we are wired to eat at every opportunity. Unable to walk past a hamburger or ice cream. After all, our Prehistoric Asshole doesn't know when the next famine is coming, and wants us to be ready, just in case. Enduring eons of scarcity has skewed it toward eating foods that will provide the highest calorie count—ones crammed with sugars and fats.

But our genes don't speak to us in words. They can't explain that they want us to eat only the highest-calorie foods in case the hunt fails miserably. To eat as much as possible through concern that it might indeed take another week to find a bison to kill. If they explained it this way, we would realize their concerns were no longer relevant to our lifestyle and could choose to ignore them.

Instead, our Prehistoric Asshole "speaks" in hormones and cravings, in taste preferences and flavors. Guiding us towards certain foods over others. Sending messages that sugar and fat are delicious. Driving our cravings for these tastes through the non-verbal, hard-wired way provided by evolution that makes fatty, sugary foods attractive to our taste buds and satiating to our bellies.

Those early humans that got the message that sugar and fat tasted *amazing* would have been driven to search out foods with high sugar and fat content. To put in more effort than other members of their clan in finding them. Getting a much-needed caloric boost to see them through hard times and providing them extra strength and energy when needed. And so, favoring them in the struggle to survive, reproduce and pass on the "I like sugar and fat genes" to the next generation.

Meantime, the obnoxious, health-conscious hipsters of the clan who kept eating kale and organic lettuce—or the equivalent healthy, pro-green, socially responsible prehistoric Whole Foods lines—missed out on the extra calories. Sure, they were ripped. But they didn't carry the excess fat that would have helped them survive without food when the hunt failed.

Without the sweet tooth, they didn't put the extra effort into finding the foods that helped them build up energy stores in their bodies. Happy instead to continue munching on shoots and leaves all day. But hey, they probably left great-looking corpses when they didn't make it through times of famine...

Any animals, including our own ancestors, that successfully found and chose high caloric food sources outlasted those that didn't. And through the rigors of natural selection, they left us today with an overblown motivation for eating. One totally out-of-proportion to the abundance and ease with which we can chow down on endless sources of fat and sugar. Today, we still carry the hard wiring of a million years. Driving us to desperately seek large quantities of high-calorie food, but without the need to exercise all day to find it.

Our hardwiring has not been updated, so our Prehistoric Asshole continues talking to us about food. All. Day. Long. Reminding us that there is still ice cream left in the freezer. *You know you love the chocolate chip. Come on, let's have some.* Or that you really deserve a hamburger and fries for lunch. That you're "dying" of hunger. *Come on,* it urges, *you can start the diet tomorrow, but you're not even going to make it until then unless you have a big feed of ribs and wings. Right. Now.*

Of course, it doesn't help that modern food producers are aware of our hardwired urge for sweet, salty, and fatty foods. Or that they use such knowledge, manipulating our innate drives to hook us in and keep us addicted to their products.[2]

Our ancestors, for instance, would have been attracted to ripe fruit with its sweet taste serving as a signal that it contained more of the valuable calories they needed. So today, food companies deliberately pump extra hidden sugar (or fat and salt) into their products. They create highly addictive junk foods by taking advantage of research showing that humans— along with many other species—respond powerfully to what have been termed supernormal stimuli. These are artificial stimuli that are deliberately bigger, brighter, or tastier than the natural stimuli they mimic.[3]

By taking a natural stimulus (in this case sugar) and doubling down on its concentration, they make sweet, brightly colored candy far more addictive than the fresh apples they mimic. Thanks, assholes . . .

What does this all mean to those of us who don't want to be dominated by an out-of-date, hairy little asshole from the Stone Age?

First, know that there is nothing wrong with you if your inner Prehistoric Asshole has influenced you to overeat. You're not bad, you're not lazy and you're not a food addict. You're human. You come with powerful, hardwired genetic coding that urges you to eat as much as you can and move as little as possible. You represent a long line of winners who knew exactly how to survive in harsh, unrelenting environments. By eating high-calorie foods every chance they had. You've beaten evolution at its own game and survived to tell the tale. Hero may seem like too strong of a word, but, I don't know . . . ?

However, now you know that it's normal to feel the urge to overeat, so you can stop wasting time beating yourself up over it. You can stop feeling like there's something wrong with you. Welcome to humanity.

Second, knowing what's going on means you no longer have to fall for the trick being played on you. Your Prehistoric Asshole's programming hasn't been updated for the last million years. It's entirely out of touch with news and current events and doesn't care that there is no longer a shortage of food - that you don't have to "earn your meal" by hunting and gathering for six hours to get a handful of berries and shoots.

It still seriously thinks you're at risk of starving "all the time." *You* know better. Remember, just because the Prehistoric Asshole feels so strongly about the matter doesn't make it so. Maybe have a handful of food at your next meal to remove your hunger, and then stop eating when you're no longer hungry, rather than when you're full. And if you don't know the difference between those two feelings—no longer being hungry vs. feeling full—there's your first project.

And most importantly, don't fall for a barrage of inner assholes ganging up on you to make you feel bad about your relationship with food. It begins with your Prehistoric Asshole tricking you into believing that you must eat or you're going to "die" of hunger. Then, after your unplanned snacking, your thoroughly modern, Instagram-influenced fat-shaming asshole joins in. Before you've had time to slink back to bed following your midnight binge raid on the peanut butter chocolate-chunk ice cream, the fat-shaming asshole is barraging you with comments like *you disgust me. You have zero self-control! Why can't you eat like a normal f*#king person!* Then another modern asshole, the healthy asshole, pipes in with, *That's it, tomorrow* *it's off to the gym! No more sugar. In fact, we might start with a 3 day fast. You can do it.* And these voices swirl around in your head as you hold your aching, stretched belly, and groan yourself to sleep in a haze of shame and guilt.

Remember, you're a hero. The OG of evolutionary success. Don't let your less well-informed inner assholes tell you otherwise. You don't have to empower any of these assholes by believing their stories. Adding a diet of shame and guilt is not the solution, nor is believing that you are somehow "less than" for having these natural drives.

The 7 Stories of the Prehistoric Asshole cont.

2. For the love of God, don't exercise!

Have you ever seen a National Geographic or David Attenborough documentary about lions? You may have noticed they enjoy a good nap (the lions, not Sir David). Sure, they hunt and eat. But as soon as they can, they're out like a light.

A sleeping lion can get a little boring after a while. So, these documentaries cut a lot of the snooze footage and focus on the action. If they didn't, pretty much all you'd see during the one-hour program is a pride of big cats sprawled about under trees. Fast asleep. For up to 20 hours a day.

Yes, you read that right, they can sleep up to 20 hours! Does that make them lazy? Should they fit in some spin classes? Go for long jogs, broken up with regular sprints to build up their cardio? No. Regardless of how little we know about wildlife in its natural habitat, we'd still find it weird if lions worked harder than they had to. Wasting energy and calories just for shits and giggles. An unlikely behavior to develop from an evolutionary perspective.

Our Prehistoric Asshole thinks this way too. That we should never do unnecessary exercise. In fact, it believes we ought to lie around as much as we can. In bed. On the couch. It doesn't matter where, as long as we're taking it easy. Why? Because for all species, conservation of energy is another hardwired adaptation. Evolving in an environment that made finding every meal a literal struggle between life and death, we know better than to be wasting those precious calories at the 7pm spin class. Instead, we conserve them, ready for the next famine.

That's why our Prehistoric Asshole is constantly coming up with excuses to get out of any type of movement that it doesn't see as necessary, productive, or enjoyable. Essentially, we are unlikely to have become wired toward any particular behavior unless there was an immediate payoff or reward. It's why getting off the couch to go down to the gym can be so damn hard. Think of the lion. Hunt. Eat. Rest. Repeat. For us, this translates to raid the freezer. Find the ice cream. Return to the couch and Netflix.

So, stop beating yourself up if you find it hard to start or stick to an exercise program. You're normal! In fact, you are fighting your evolutionary programming. Don't be so hard on yourself. But also, don't make excuses such as *I'm flawed,* or *I just don't have as much willpower as the next person.* Know that if others are sticking to an exercise program, they've had to overcome the same challenges. Meaning you can too. Especially after you've learned how to own your internal dialog in the coming chapters.

The 7 Stories of the Prehistoric Asshole cont.

3. I deserve better and more . . .

There's a wonderful clip on YouTube showing a couple of Capuchin monkeys given a task—to hand a small pebble to a researcher when she puts her palm out. Google "Capuchin monkey wants more" to take a look.

If the monkeys pass the researcher a pebble from the small pile in their cages, she gives them either a piece of cucumber or a grape as reward. Like humans, these monkeys have evolved to seek foods with higher calorie counts, meaning they value grapes over cucumber.

In this experiment, each monkey is in its own cage, side by side and in full view of the other. Monkey A (I don't know their real names) is the first to give a pebble to the researcher and receive a piece of cucumber in return. Perfectly satisfied with the result, Monkey A eats the cucumber. The researcher then receives a pebble from Monkey B. Instead of cucumber, however, she passes Monkey B a grape.

Monkey A sees this . . .

The researcher repeats the process with Monkey A. The pebble is received, and another piece of cucumber is handed over. Followed by all hell breaking loose as Monkey A throws a fit, tossing the cucumber at the researcher's head, jumping up and down, pounding its fists on the cage and bench. It seems cucumber no longer cuts it as a reward. Realizing that juicy grapes are available, that's all it wants from now on.

Meet what I call the voice of the grabby asshole. Grabby always wants more. Grabby represents the joy of desire. Think of this circuit in the brain—running on dopamine for fuel—as your "wanting circuit." It makes perfect sense that such a drive provided a selective advantage to our prehistoric ancestors. After all, prehistoric humans who were driven to seek greater food security, better shelter, or ways to make stronger, sharper tools would have been well placed for survival against competitors who didn't.

However, striving for more can be hard work. And that's where the "wanting circuit" comes in. Its job is to make sure we maintain motivation; to keep us moving forward. Making sure we're never satisfied with what we've got, and constantly fueling our fear of missing out.

Our dopamine circuits make sure desire and pleasure-seeking always feels good. It doesn't matter what it is, as long as it's more. We daydream for hours, days, even years about bigger, better, more expensive things. Just got yourself a nice car? Sure, you're happy with it for a while, but before you know it, you're taking it for granted. It no longer makes you feel good the way it did when you first took delivery. Now you want a better one. Love your new house? Give it a while. Eventually, you'll think you want something bigger and better. Got a good job? Now you need a better job . . . and on it goes.

An out-of-control "wanting circuit," super-stimulated by 21st-century consumer society and social media, leaves our inner Prehistoric Asshole forever "hungry" for more. *Why should I put up with cucumbers when there are grapes out there?*

Adding to the challenge is another sweet irony. That our "wanting circuit" is entirely different from our "liking circuit." Meaning we can really crave something, but then when we finally get it, we don't like it as much as we thought we would. For instance, a friend told me recently how all they'd wanted was to be in a relationship. But now they're in one, all they notice on social media is how their single friends are out having such a great time. And they wish they could be out there with them, chasing the same good time.

The grape always looks so much greener on the other side . . .

At a personal level, I realized how I was doing precisely the same sort of thing a few years ago. Despite experiencing a windfall profit from the successful sale of a company I had helped grow. With enough cash to give up work, buy a nice home, an expensive car, and spend around 6-8 months each year traveling for leisure around the planet. And not least of all, having enough money left over to buy a few businesses that would keep paying me a passive income. Forever.

Yet, I still wanted more. Why wasn't my home a little bigger? Sure, I had river views, but I could have a nicer view of the skyline, right? And yes, my car is nice, but the new Mercedes models look pretty good too . . .

It's ridiculous when I read those last few paragraphs back to myself. What a jerk. And yet, it reflects a powerful truth about human nature. That no matter how successful we are, and no matter what we have, we always want more. The cycle of desire, fleeting happiness, dissatisfaction, and disappointment simply resets and begins again. With our prehistoric grabby asshole high on dopamine, telling us that everything will be ok if we just get to those greener grapes. Then we'll feel better . . .

———

I HAVE FOUND the first step to beating this innate human drive is awareness. For example, when I notice the familiar pattern of my grabby asshole telling me that my apartment would be perfect, *if only* . . . if only the living area was a little bigger . . . you know, maybe a few feet wider. Then it would be perfect.

When I hear this voice, I call it out for what it is. Absolute bull-shit! Simply the voice of an inner asshole that always wants more. And while it may always be there (I'm only human), it doesn't need to control me, my happiness, or my decisions. I can laugh it off knowing that if I found an apartment a few feet wider, there would just be something else next time that my inner asshole would "if only" me about.

Now, I remind myself about just how lucky I am. How grateful I am to have enough in my life to share with others. And that very act of thinking about others—focusing outwardly rather than on self—changes everything. It brings genuine joy to the present moment, intersecting as it does with my other legitimate, hardwired needs such as meaning and connection.

The 7 Stories of the Prehistoric Asshole cont.

4. Be quick to anger but slow to find happiness . . .

Have you noticed that it doesn't take a lot to make a person angry, but it can be really tough to cheer them up? This can't be helpful, right? Yet there are several hardwired reasons for our bias toward anger over happiness, that have served us well as a species for millions of years.

So, what is the evolutionary benefit of being an angry asshole? How does our salty inner asshole think it's helping us?

One scientific explanation, The Recalibrational Theory of Anger, proposes that we are hardwired through natural selection to get angry as a bargaining tactic. That anger can be used to get our way with others when we want or need something. It proposes that anger skews others towards giving in and provides adaptive advantages to those who use it.

It works like this: Imagine you have just been approached by an angry person furiously demanding that you hand over the $1.00 soda in your hand. At this point, you have to decide. Do you get into a fight with this clearly angry and seemingly irrational person who is insistent that you hand over your soda? Or do you just hand it over? Is the $1.00 replacement cost worth the risk of injury?

Research shows that many people decide getting rid of the "soda-can-nut-job" is indeed worth the $1.00 loss. Particularly those at a power disadvantage—for instance, the angry person is bigger and scarier looking than they are. Especially if there's no one around to tip the balance of power back in their favor. Sorry, there's no cop on this corner . . .

Under these circumstances, a display of anger changes your perspective on the relative merits of "negotiation." It changes how you weigh up the "value" of the soda to the angry person and what they may be willing to do to get it.

Imagine instead that an equally random stranger approached you, smiling harmlessly, asking if they could have your can of soda. Without the demonstration of anger and the resulting inference of a) the soda's high value to the person asking for it and b) the potential harm from the implied threat that anger signals, you are far more likely to ignore or refuse the request.

That's The Recalibrational Theory of Anger at work. Underpinning an unconscious awareness that others will often give in to excessively emotional demands rather than deal with the fallout of a "no." A message that every toddler learns from an early age as their parents cave in to demands for, well, whatever, to avoid yet another exhausting tantrum . . .

Anger also serves as a signal to others that a "line" has been crossed, providing a measure of protection from actual harm by scaring off possible attackers before anyone actually gets hurt. For the person getting angry, it also provides a survival advantage by triggering the release of adrenaline within their body. Once released into the bloodstream, adrenaline causes increases in heart rate, blood pressure and sugar metabolism— boosting energy and muscle strength throughout the body. Ready for fight club, circa 50,000BC.

All of this makes anger an alluring siren song for the Prehistoric Asshole. Angry asshole is ready to show up at a moment's notice to let the world know that you're not happy. And it is quick to show up because the triggers that set it off in prehistoric times were urgent "do or die" situations that required immediate action. A member of another clan trying to take your can of soda; a predator blocking the path. With hesitation seen as a sign of weakness, we evolved a hair-trigger, adrenaline-inspired anger display, ready to scare off potential offenders.

Unfortunately, today the offender is a harmless grandmother blocking traffic with her cautious driving. During peak hour. *Peak hour folks.* Triggering the angry asshole in the heads of the drivers stuck behind her. *Who drives like this?!* it screams. *Why would granny come out in the middle of peak hour? Doesn't she know the rest of us need to get to work? Why can't she pull over and let the serious people get their shit done?! WTF!* We get angry, the adrenaline courses through our veins. Before we know it, we're overtaking dangerously into oncoming traffic, screaming abuse, and flipping off poor old granny . . .

MEANWHILE, happiness seems hard to find and even harder to hold on to. Just as there are reasons we're hardwired towards anger to solve our problems, the difficulty in finding happiness also makes evolutionary sense. Despite most people's stated preference for happiness, there is little to suggest that it provided any clear and urgent survival advantage to our ancestors. In fact, it's been argued that unhappiness was a more useful emotional state for our prehistoric ancestors, because it motivated them to make changes. In contrast, happiness was at best a subtle and indirect drive.

Walking around happily all the time may have even been dangerous for our prehistoric ancestors. Imagine the "half-glass-full" prehistoric stoner that always reacted with a grin on his face no matter what the situation. Dangerous enemies approaching the camp? *No problem, I'm sure we can talk it out with them,* he tells himself. River running dry. *Don't worry, I'm sure it will rain soon . . . no need to pack up camp and go looking for greener pastures . . .* Yeah, I'm betting this dude died of thirst nursing a spear sticking out of his butt . . .

In this way, it's thought that the "happy-the-way-things-are" ancestors may have been less competitive. Leaving them outmaneuvered by the more vigilant, cagey, and quick-to-anger —or violence—types. Which meant they didn't get to pass on their "I'm so happy" genes to subsequent generations. Keep this process going for a million or so years, and you get us. A bunch of suspicious, marginally satisfied, rarely happy bunch of humans with twitchy trigger fingers.

All of which gives us yet more reason to work on recalibrating how these inner voices influence us. After all, why let prehistoric drivers that are no longer relevant to modern life continue making us miserable?

The 7 Stories of the Prehistoric Asshole cont.

5. Revenge is sweet . . .

We have all wished we could "get even" at one time or another
in our lives. And if not in a position to get even ourselves,
maybe we have soothed ourselves by hoping one day the
Universe, Karma, God's punishment, or something, would get
even for us. Stick it to "them" for their transgressions; teach
them a thing or two for whatever it is they have done wrong.

Yes, revenge is a universal emotion, thought to emanate from
deep in our psychological past. Considered by many
researchers amongst the strongest of human emotions, along-
side love, anger, fear, and grief. Within tribal settings, revenge
acts as a signal that you are not someone to be crossed lightly. It
is also used to maintain a primitive justice system; to keep
order. Think of the Old Testament's guideline for punishment,
a " . . . life for a life, eye for an eye, tooth for tooth, soda can for
soda can . . . "

Revenge to get "justice" was a common recourse across many
tribal cultures. It is still widely practiced across the world today
wherever the nation-state is weak, and local groups take "justice" into their own hands. While some psychologists and
researchers argue that those who take revenge can feel the
worse for it in the long run, others have shown evidence for
even greater remorse or regret by those who did not take the
opportunity for revenge when it was available. Suffice to say, no
matter how ugly an emotion it may be, it has been—and still is
—widely practiced, commonly felt, and as "normal" as any of
our other hardwired emotions.

All that said, as Martin Luther King Jr observed, "the old law of
'an eye for an eye' leaves everybody blind." Our mindful self

gets it. Living in an environment where life has become an endless cycle of revenge between enemies is no life at all.

Taking revenge into one's own hands—no matter how sweet the Prehistoric Asshole tells you it will feel—leaves a trail of destruction and ongoing violence for all. The ability to forgive, understand and move on from situations where we feel wronged—be it a family member, lover, colleague, or stranger—is one of the most challenging things we must do. It may also be one of the healthiest steps we can take for ourselves.

The 7 Stories of the Prehistoric Asshole cont.

6. Be afraid. Be very afraid . . .

You might remember the story of Barry and Forrest from the second chapter. It explains why assuming something scary is happening—for example, that a movement in the bushes might be a lion—provides an evolutionary advantage. With the ensuing release of adrenaline within the frightened person's body leading to increased energy and muscle strength, and so priming them for fight or flight.

This adaptive advantage of feeling fear is no longer relevant for the average person living in a modern environment. Our prehistoric ancestors could work off their adrenaline surge through the physical exertion of running or fighting to resolve issues that triggered their fear. Today, our fear is triggered by things that we cannot fight to the ground or spear in the chest. Instead of providing an advantage, the release of adrenaline just makes us sweat profusely and stumble over our words as we ask that person we like in the spin class out on a date.

Your boss' angry look, the news that the IRS is looking into your tax affairs, or the increasing cost of groceries may all be cause for fear. But unlike the risks faced by our ancestors, these are not the type that come bursting out of the bushes unexpectedly. Instead, they creep up on you. These types of concerns are incremental, unrelenting, and often have no immediate resolution. They leave you simmering in your own juices, a poisonous cocktail of hormones that raises your blood pressure, increases your heart rate, and makes you feel a sense of free-floating anxiety. Leaving you one final straw away from retreating into a depressed ball of sorrow or "going postal."

These persistent, slow-burning versions of fear and stress are significant issues for mental health in today's world, often leading to depression and anxiety. For now, though, just remember when facing these emotions that you are not alone. You are experiencing the most universal of feelings. And there is hope.

The 7 Stories of the Prehistoric Asshole cont.

7. Of course you should feel Jealous . . .

We've all experienced the uncomfortable sting of the green-eyed monster at some stage in our lives—its poison bringing on a range of symptoms, from vague discomfort to heart-piercing pain—driving insecurity, anger, and all manner of ugliness. It is often triggered in the blink of an eye. Maybe the work colleague who received that promotion you thought you deserved. The neighbor who bought a ridiculously nice car (I mean, how do they afford that, right?). Or maybe your partner interacting with the just-a-little-too-friendly, kind of hot, work friend at the end-of-year office party.

Jealousy and its close cousin—envy—are two more emotions hardwired into our inner Prehistoric Asshole. Both involve a subject or target seen to be better off than you are. Strictly defined, jealousy revolves around the perception of someone taking what you already have. While envy is felt when you want something that someone else has. You're envious of the neighbor's expensive new car. Jealous of the colleague who's definitely flirting with your partner. At times, the words are used interchangeably to identify that gut feeling; that gnawing sensation of seeing what others have that you don't. And wanting your slice.

Our inner Prehistoric Asshole is quick to tell us how unfair things are when we see others with "more", "bigger", or "better" than us. In addition, social media is now serving as a constant reminder that everyone else is having more fun than we are. Bigger parties, better holidays, nicer clothes, more friends and more "likes." Instead of bringing us closer together, social media is leaving us feeling isolated, unsuccessful, and with a sense that we have less to be happy about in our lives.[4]

This compulsion for comparison has a solid evolutionary link to behavior that provided an adaptive advantage to our long-forgotten prehistoric ancestors. In hunter-gatherer settings, being on guard for the "fair" sharing of resources, and strongly driven to doing something about it when another member of the tribe hogged more than their fair share of the goodies, made good sense. This resource competition within the tribe—be it for food, shelter, or other scarce resources—required the development of an acute sense for keeping tabs on their allocation.

The growth of an emotion such as envy—to drive behavior that might balance the scales when we felt someone had more than us—could be the difference between life and death under such circumstances. Jealousy related to our sexual partners could have provided similar adaptive advantages to our prehistoric ancestors, making us more protective of those with whom we had mated or those we wished to. This trait improved the likelihood of our DNA passing on to the next generation, instead of the DNA of that overly-friendly guy from the cave next door.

Our prehistoric ancestors who felt greater envy or jealousy were more strongly driven to out-perform their less jealous competitors, perpetuating and increasing the strength of these emotions as they were reinforced over successive generations. The evolution of these behaviors has left us today with a distressed and resentful prehistoric inner asshole. One that becomes obsessed with personal "injustice" when others do better.

Knowing where this particular obsession of the inner asshole comes from provides clues to how we can rethink our approach to such feelings. As hard as it seems, it may be time to stop comparing ourselves to others. Or to at least recognize that what we see of other's lives is not always the truth.

Take what you see on social media; carefully curated images designed to show the very best, the most exciting moments of that person's life. Ideally captured using a selfie stick for the most flattering angle. Not the other ninety percent of their life —the boring stuff, the arguments, the tears, and regret. Everyone has their own personal demons, inadequacies, and fears, whether you see it in their social media stream or not. And guess what, they are probably busy feeling envious of someone else's posts, someone they think has more . . .

If you are going to make comparisons, practice comparing with the people coming up behind you, rather than those who seem to be out "in front." Maybe start by thinking of those who are materially worse off than you; the close to one billion people who live in extreme poverty and go hungry daily. Perhaps the ones in your own county, your own city or neighborhood that have so much less. Start by asking yourself, is there anything I could do for them? Could helping others who have less than I, shift my focus powerfully and positively? Away from the envious asshole within, toward a state of gratitude for what I already have?

Try spending a few minutes each day reflecting on what you can be grateful for in your life. Perhaps think of one new thing each day and keep doing this for 21 days. Research has shown that cultivating gratitude in this way—by changing the story you tell yourself—is positively related to enhanced well-being.[5]

It's a choice. To stop and smell the roses, or to keep getting pissed at the person who got a bigger bouquet than you on Valentine's Day . . .

But trust me, unless you choose a different path, it never stops. The comparison that drives jealousy and envy will always be with you, for-f@#king-ever. Because no matter what you have, there will always be someone with more. A bigger paycheck, nicer car, or a better zip code.

Don't fall for it.

When the inner voice of envy comes calling, focus on gratitude and scrap the comparisons.

The Prehistoric inner asshole . . . A Recap

Let's recap the main points we have established are useful to know about the hardwired inner voice that we've called the Prehistoric Asshole.

This voice and its messages result from millions of years of a game called survival of the fittest. It is the voice of those individuals who outwitted, outplayed, and outlasted their competitors for the opportunity to live long enough to mate, have children and pass their genes—their "programming"—onto future generations.

Specific "programming" that gave certain individuals a winning edge in this game, survival of the fittest, was in turn concentrated over time to become dominant traits for the species that has developed into the modern human. If eating at every opportunity, not exercising more than necessary, getting angry, jealous, sad, or seeking revenge were winning moves (and they were), then these traits became dominant in our species.

If being on edge, cautious, somewhat fearful, or anxious helped them avoid being eaten by predators, then these traits were also likely to dominate over time. These attributes came to be hardwired like a blueprint for the physical and psychological characteristics that would make someone a winner in the world of hunter-gathering.

Let's be clear, there's nothing wrong with these traits. They serve a purpose under certain circumstances even today, and absolutely did so in our prehistoric environment. But, and it's a big butt (see what I did there, it's an ass joke in a book all about assholes . . .), these same traits can be destructive too. Especially when used outside the environment in which they developed.

And that's the situation we find ourselves in today. Living in a 21st-century culture equipped with prehistoric instructions for how to think, act and feel. Feeling the urge to eat when we no longer need to; resisting exercise when it would be a good idea; worrying about stuff that we know we shouldn't but just can't seem to help; and getting angry, jealous, and sad in ways that no longer help us succeed but instead make us sick or dysfunctional.

We are all in the same boat. The person you think doesn't have these sorts of problems, with voices and urges to be lazy, eat crap or get angry, is the person you just don't know well enough yet. Or who's lying to you, themselves, or both.

The most important thing to realize is that these out-of-date, bossy "rules of the game" are just a normal by-product of our evolution. They're not "wrong," and we're not "bad" for having them. It's just one of those things about being human. And beating yourself up over it will only make it worse.

Instead, let's learn how to rewrite our stories; talk our inner assholes down from the ledge and lead happier lives. Our next mission is to learn about a few other inner asshole voices that have developed more recently than the Prehistoric Asshole.

***

References

1. Burnett, C.J., Li, C., Webber, E., Tsaousidou, E., Xue, S.Y., Brüning, J.C., Krashes, M.J., (2016). Hunger-Driven Motivational State Competition, Neuron, 92 (1), 187-201

2. Goodwin, B.C., Browne, M., Rockloff, M. (2015). Measuring Preference for Supernormal Over Natural Rewards: A Two-Dimensional Anticipatory Pleasure Scale, Evolutionary Psychology.

3. Deirdre Barrett (2010). *Supernormal Stimuli: How Primal Urges Overran Their Evolutionary Purpose*, Norton agency titles.

4. Dhir, A., Yossatorn, Y., Kaur, Chen, S. (2018). Online social media fatigue and psychological wellbeing—A study of

compulsive use, fear of missing out, fatigue, anxiety and depression. International Journal of Information Management. 40, 141-152.

5. Alex M. Wood, A.M., Froh, J.J., Geraghty, A.W.A., (2010). Gratitude and well-being: A review and theoretical integration, Clinical Psychology Review, Nov; 30 (7):890-905

8

THE BULLYING ASSHOLE

The inner Bullying Asshole contains voices of parents and authority figures stuck in our heads, taking up space rent-free, and still telling us what we should and shouldn't do with our lives. Shaming and blaming at every turn should we—or others—stray from the "rules" or fail to live up to various expectations sculptured by our parents and society.

Our Bullying Asshole is filled with judgments, values, and attitudes; constantly telling us how we must behave to be accepted; adamant in reminding us of the "right way to do things." This is the inner asshole that can be heard telling you to never admit you're wrong; you can't trust anyone; or you need to lose weight if you want someone to love you.

Real crap. Crap that can bruise and stunt relationships, results, and lives.

The problem is we absorb this conditioning in the first few years of life. Way before we can reflect on whether the rules and attitudes of our parents or those around us are beneficial, positive, or life-affirming. As such, these unfiltered imperatives are full of "nasties"; rules and comments that are limiting, destructive, or wounding in nature.

The Inner Bully also lacks context or sensible instruction for when its rules are to be used and how they are to be applied. So, we find ourselves at age 33 still being told by our inner voice to leave nothing on our plate and feeling guilty if we do. Despite being full and not feeling like eating any more of what's left in front of us.

Often one-dimensional and oversimplified in nature, these rules and principles are expected to be followed because your parents or authority figures "told you so." Frighteningly, they come not only from parental and authority figures but also the television, media, and video games to which we're exposed in those early years.

Suppose, for instance, your inner bully forms under the heavy influence of how John Wick or The Godfather (parts one, two, and three) deal with their problems. And that these values are then reinforced by your actual parents' behaviors. Leaving you absorbing some disturbing rules about how to face down challenges as an adult.

For the rest of your life, you end up blindly following a set of rules that are never "fact-checked" on the way in. And never re-examined for relevance, truth, or usefulness once you've matured sufficiently to do so.

Instead, your Bullying Asshole keeps parroting what is heard as a 3-year-old over and over in your ear. Some of it useful and some downright poisonous.

"Brush your teeth before bed," (good).

"Stand up straight," (sure).

"Never back down," (well, let's think about that . . . are you related to John Wick?).

"Real men don't cry," (hang on a minute . . .).

"Don't touch yourself," (hmm, but . . .).

Your Bullying Asshole is triggered into many actions hundreds of times a day as you navigate relationships, work, and social interactions. Easier than conscious, thoughtful dialog, or being mindful and truly present for others, the Bullying Asshole has a rule or play-sheet for every interaction.

Easily spotted, these conditioned responses usually come as absolutes, delivered in the way a parent might instruct a child. Full of *should* and *should nots*; *have to's*; *can't*; *never's*; and *always* statements. In this way, the inner Bully falls back on a barrage of judgmental language and critical words, patronizing those around you in the way it delivers advice and instructions.

When turned inwards, your Bullying Asshole is the voice telling you that you "must" do one thing or another, or else you'll go to hell, never succeed, or no one will love you. Spewing its opinions throughout the day, one "rule" or judgment after another. It may even come as a specific memory of a time when a parental figure actually said some of these things to you. A memory of a voice still loaded with the venom and pain it produced twenty years ago, hitting repeat every time it's triggered by current circumstances.

No one will love you if you're too fat, it tells you as you eat, triggering a bout of shame.

Don't let the pushy bastards in, it snarls in your ear as the driver next to you tries to merge lanes in heavy traffic.

Never talk back. It just makes things worse . . . it warns you as your partner tries to engage in conversation about a relationship problem.

In this way, we end up allowing ourselves to be bullied by parts of ourselves that have nothing stronger in terms of weapons than harsh words and disapproval. So many judgments, rules, and opinions soaked up by each generation . . . and then mindlessly passed on when their turn as parents comes along.

The Bullying Asshole, armed with the authority of years of unchallenged childhood conditioning, can be a lifetime in the unmaking. It is, however, a project worth undertaking if we are to live our best life.

The first and perhaps most empowering thing we can do is to pause as we hear the Bullying Asshole speak up. Pause and recognize it for what it is—an asshole. By doing this—calling it out—we disempower its bullshit. It can still get in our ear, but we don't have to let it run the show.

For example, I use this approach while driving. Specifically, when there is a case of "bad" driving (other people's, of course, never mine . . .). This can often be a trigger for my Bullying Asshole to arc up. *Why aren't they using their f@#king turn signals?* it yells as the car in front changes lanes. *Idiots that are too stupid to drive properly shouldn't be allowed on the road*, it mutters in my ear. *Give them the horn Darryl, do it, do it*, it insists.

This is the type of stuff that I can spot now for what it is—bullshit. Courtesy of the Bullying Asshole. I know it's not how I really feel if I check in with my mindful self. And it's certainly not how I'd act if I were living my best self. As soon as I come to realize this pattern, I find it easy to laugh at myself—at how ridiculous my Bullying Asshole is being.

After all, why get bent out of shape by something so simple, so ordinary, and so unimportant? Do I really think I'm the boss of everyone? At this point, realizing what a jerk my Bullying Asshole is being, I remind myself to pull my head out of my ass and stop acting as if someone put me in charge of the traffic system. Life is too short.

My Bullying Asshole may get the first word in, but I recognize it for being that—an ass—and have a good laugh at it instead. Job done. No going down-the- rabbit-hole of expletives and frustration about other road users. Anger that does nothing but increases my chances of a stroke or heart attack before I even get to work . . .

9

THE DAMAGED ASSHOLE

Mason had been single for six months when he met Emma.

Chatting regularly at the local coffee shop each morning on the way to their respective jobs; he finally worked up the courage to ask for her number. He was a little surprised and altogether thrilled when she passed it to him without hesitation. Before he knew it, they were messaging regularly about nothing in particular.

After a few days, Mason decided it was time to take the plunge and ask her out. After all, what could go wrong? They liked each other . . . right? He sent the message, knowing Emma usually responded within a few minutes at most. He waited. And waited. Long minutes dragged by. He felt sick somewhere deep in the pit of his stomach. Did he say something wrong he wondered, as he opened and scrutinized the message repeatedly? Had he screwed up? Been too pushy? Or maybe the message didn't go through? Perhaps there was a fault in the network . . . *should I send another?* Emotions and nagging self-doubts swirled out of control. *Why can't she just reply??* he asked himself.

Mason's Damaged Asshole had been triggered.

We all took damage growing up. It may have been verbal, emotional, or physical. Even under the best of circumstances, sometimes our three-year-old self—unable to understand the nuances of the adults around us—was left feeling isolated, hurt, abandoned, or unloved.

The Damaged Asshole is the voice of this vast collection of wounded feelings from our childhood years, along with stories we created to make sense of the situations we found ourselves in. Haunting us with all the times we felt unsafe, judged, or "not enough" as a small child. When we were too young to work things out or to "use our words" to explain our feelings. Instead, we got upset, stormed off, or sulked. For these were the only strategies available to our three-year-old brains to process our distress.

We may have also created stories to make sense of our pain. *I've been bad. No wonder mom and dad are never happy around me.* Leading to *it's my fault dad left us* . . . when our parents split. Horrible, misinformed stories fabricated by our three-year-old brain to make sense of the world around it. And carried forward as guilt and shame—by the Damaged Asshole—into our adult lives.

Much of this psychic material is stored unconsciously, leaving us confused as adults as to why the judgment of others can seem so terrifying; or why we feel so utterly abandoned when a loved one gives us "that look" of disapproval. Or perhaps why we're driven by the need for acceptance by certain people or institutions. This is the Damaged Asshole still alive in all of us, primed, loaded, and ready to go off whenever our insecurities are triggered. Ready to drag us through precisely the same emotional responses learned over those first few years of life. A thin-skinned, emotionally maladjusted asshole that's always one criticism, one wrong look, or one perceived mistake away from regressing to when we were three years old.

And that's what was going on for Mason. He felt sick in the stomach as butterflies swirled, feelings of rejection and loneliness bubbling up, fueled by self-doubt. Before he knew what was happening, Mason was in the grip of the Damaged Asshole. He couldn't concentrate on anything else, checking his messages every few moments in case he'd missed something.

The Damaged Asshole's grip can seem impossible to break. Completely taking over the mind's operating system, leaving us to see and feel the world through the emotional eyes of our upset three-year-old.

You shouldn't have used the heart emoji. It was too soon! it admonished, slapping its imaginary forehead with a silent Homer Simpson's *D'oh!*

You appeared too needy. Now she'll think you're desperate, it mumbled.

What's wrong with you!? it demanded to know.

Such a f@#king loser . . . nothing ever works out . . . But before it could finish that line of insult, the familiar "ding" of a message arriving on the phone interrupted the Damaged Asshole.

Mason scrambled to read it. "Sorry, been driving, couldn't text. Would love to go on a date!" the message read. In less than a second, Mason's mood changed to joy and excitement. All was forgiven and forgotten as the spotlight of attention swung away from the performance being given by the Damaged Asshole.

The Damaged Asshole had gotten what it needed—confirmation that Mason was, in fact, worthy of interest, affection and connection—affirmation that someone cared. And instantly, he felt great.

This whirlwind of drama all brought to us courtesy of the Damaged Asshole. Talking to us in ways that make us feel like, well, shit.

Saying things like:

- *It's all my fault.*
- *Nobody loves me.*
- *I'll never find someone to be with.*
- *Why can't I do anything right?*
- *Why is everything so hard?*
- *I'm so stupid.*
- *I can't take it.*
- *F@#k my life.*
- *Just kill me.*
- *I can't do it.*
- *Everything is falling apart.*
- *It's too hard.*
- *They're all talking about me.*

These statements are all signs of an activated Damaged Asshole. A way of talking that signifies giving up, blaming ourselves for everything, and led by the "overwhelm" of the 3-year-old you. Its language is always taken to an extreme, full of "woe is me," "isn't it awful," "nobody understands what I'm going through" type shit. Triggering feelings of doubt and sadness; leaving us soaking in fear and loneliness, feeling like we'll never be enough.

Worse still, we don't just relive all of these feelings and beliefs whilst in the grip of the Damaged Ass; we fall for the idea that our exaggerated and unrestrained reactions are caused by the person in front of us at the time. We blame our boss, our partner, or our kids for making us sad or angry. We need instead to realize and accept these reactions belong to us, not them; *our* pain is based on *our* stuff. These reactions are already inside us when we walk into a room. Lurking just below the surface, ready to be triggered. A childhood's worth of pain, projected onto the next unlucky sap that does the "wrong" thing . . .

Take, for example, giving a small suggestion to a colleague at work about an email they wrote. Instead of their mindful self reflecting on the feedback, they burst into tears as they ask, "why do you think everything I do is shit?" An example of the Damaged Ass taking control. Or maybe they come out swinging, shouting angrily, and demanding "Who do you think you are to criticize me!?" An example of the Bullying Asshole going on the attack. Either response, completely out of proportion to the feedback that "perhaps you can drop the double space after each period in your emails." Out of proportion because they aren't *really* responding to the feedback about their punctuation skills. Instead, they're responding to the emotionally charged spillover resulting from their Damaged Asshole being triggered, reminding them of every time they did something wrong or got into trouble as a little kid.

This cycle of something, anything, triggering the inner Damaged Asshole—resulting in a rerun of out-of-proportion feelings of unhappiness—is a real and present danger to our lives. Imagine perhaps the arrival of an unexpected credit card bill, triggering the Damaged Asshole's feelings of hopelessness. Immediately, we start to see everything through the lens of fear and inadequacy. A heavy blanket of anxiety cloaks everything around us, and suddenly the whole day looks dark and gloomy.

No matter where we look, we can now find more things to stress over. No matter the news, it is heard by a part of us that feels bad about anything, because everything is a reminder that we're not good enough. Time for lunch? *Great, just gonna get fatter,* our inner Damaged Asshole retorts as it tries to eat its emotions. Worked out how to pay the credit card bill? All that does is give the Damaged Asshole more ammunition to remind us of what a close call it was; that we're a victim; and that it might not work out next time.

The key to dealing with this asshole is to recognize it is driven by its damage and its wounds. And that it learned its strategies for dealing with the world when you were just two or three-years-old—before you grew a rational brain—back when your only tools in the face of setbacks were sulking and screaming. So you can't expect a rational response from it now.

Like a two or three-year-old, it just wants to know that everything will be okay. To be accepted and understood. So, be kind to yourself. Recognize, when you are angry or sad, these feelings are clues something is coming up *for you.* Don't blame the people who happen to trigger these feelings. They are *yours,* own them. You're the only one who can change how you relate to them.

10

COGNITIVE DISTORTIONS. THE LANGUAGE OF ASSHOLES

Dan's Story

Brought to you by Dan's inner asshole.

Examples of cognitive distortions in bold italics.

Y *ou've had a really, really hard day,* the voice whispered in Dan's ear. *Anybody would have a few drinks after a day like this; you deserve it.* Dan's face twisted in conflict. He'd promised himself not to drink today. He was three days into a month-long challenge to go "dry." He wanted to prove to himself that he didn't **need** the couple of drinks (well, maybe it was more than that, perhaps five or six) he had each night at the corner bar on the way home. *I'll still pop in there,* he told himself, but just for the company, to catch up with the friends he had made.

And that's how the bender started . . .

It was days like this Dan found hardest. When he'd had a tough time at work. And his inner voice seemed to know exactly what to say: *You've had a **really** hard day. Just one **can't** hurt. You **deserve** it. They're your friends. You **should** at least stop by the bar and see them.*

Your inner asshole seems to know just what to say to get inside your head. Probably because it's been there the whole time. It knows your weaknesses, your hopes, and fears. Which carrots to dangle, and which sticks to hit you with. It's the "cheerleader" for bad choices, masquerading as the voice of reason. Telling you it's right to feel weak, lost, or without hope; that the problems in front of you are too large, too scary, or too much to bear. Why it's ok to have that second serving of cake, you know, just this last time before starting your diet tomorrow . . .

Our Inner Asshole, the great exaggerator

It's this ability to make our weaknesses and desires seem more compelling than they are that makes the inner asshole so dangerous. As the ultimate manipulator of information, it takes the short-sighted concerns and desires of a part of us that's been left in the dark, that has no idea of reality, and makes them believable. The fears of the Damaged Asshole or the judgment of the Bullying Asshole are magnified. The desires of our most childish parts are made irresistible.

We convince ourselves we just *can't* live without the extra piece of cake, the latest model smartphone, or the most on-trend fashion item on eBay. The inner asshole takes the worst of our shit from childhood, gives it a polish, sprinkles it with a bit of glitter, and tries to convince us that the steaming pile of caca is good for us . . .

And in this way, it attempts to convince you of complete and utter bullshit.

That *nobody* will *ever* love you.

That you're *never* going to make *it.*

That you *have* to buy that new . . . (insert name of any item you needed more than life itself until you got it, and now sits unused in the garage).

All the words in bolded italics are examples of these exaggerations and manipulations—designed by the inner asshole for maximum impact on your psyche and emotions.

How does this type of language make things worse? Say, for instance, you don't get the promotion at work that you've been working towards. This is a once-off setback to your plans. But rather than see the problem in those terms, the inner asshole tells you something like *you're **never** going to get promoted.* Presenting a single setback as if it were something permanent. No wonder you get upset after that.

These italicized words are examples of the simple yet cunning wordplay, flawed logic, and misdirection used by the inner asshole. Yet your bullshit detector probably didn't go off when you read them. These language patterns of deception, distortion, and confusion are so commonplace that you don't even notice them in everyday life. That's why they work. Because they slip straight past your usual defenses, convincing you of all sorts of debilitating crap. Leaving you to fall for these fundamental errors in how to think about yourself, others, and life in general.

In therapy, these patterns are considered dangerous. Left unchecked, they diminish you and leave you feeling unworthy. Instead, let's learn to spot them and use them as "red flags" for your mindful self to be on alert for incoming crap. And once spotted, to act as triggers for you to apply various strategies for ridding yourself of their influence over your life.

Welcome to the world of Cognitive Distortions

---

cognitive distortion [kog-ni-tiv] [dih-stawr-shuhn]

1. an exaggerated or irrational thought pattern involved in the onset or perpetuation of psychopathological states, such as depression and anxiety.

2. thoughts that cause individuals to perceive reality inaccurately.

3. *the way our inner assholes f@#k with us.*

Cognitive distortions are the lingua franca of our inner assholes, the common language used to tell us their stories. These distortions make our weaknesses and desires seem more compelling and our fears and anxieties more extreme. Providing a "backdoor" into the feeling brain, making everything seem more real, more important, or more alarming. And they make us sick with anxiety, fear, and sadness.

But maybe you're thinking, *how much harm can the way I talk to myself really do? I mean, they're just words, right?*

Wrong. So f@#king wrong! And if you don't believe me, let's ask *Science!*

Cognitive Distortions. Science says they're really, really bad.

Just look at this small selection of headline findings from respected medical journals, researching the impact of cognitive distortions on our health and wellbeing.

. . .

PARTICIPANTS with Major Depressive Disorder have higher levels of cognitive distortion. From "An investigation of different aspects of overgeneralization in patients with major depressive disorder and borderline personality disorder," the British Journal of Clinical Psychology, 2012.

PARTICIPANTS WHO HAD RECENTLY ATTEMPTED suicide are more likely to experience cognitive distortions. From "Cognitive Distortions and Suicide Attempts" in the journal Cognitive Therapy and Research, 2014.

THERE IS A SIGNIFICANT, positive correlation between ADHD and cognitive distortions. From "Assessment of the relationship between self-reported cognitive distortions and adult ADHD, anxiety, depression, and hopelessness," in the journal "Psychiatry Research," 2016.

COGNITIVE DISTORTIONS ARE ASSOCIATED with elevated depressive symptoms. From "Cognitive Distortions, Humor Styles, and Depression," Europe's Journal of Psychology, 2016.

What we say to ourselves really matters . . . and how we say it can cause actual harm . . .

Unpacking Cognitive Distortions

So, what are these tricks? These hidden language patterns that twist the truth, exaggerate how bad things are, and tie us up in a perverted logic that will always justify feeling worse than we need, for no good reason?

Before we unpack these routines, keep one crucial thing in mind: Your inner assholes are not just misleading, they are slippery bastards as well.

As we review each routine, you might hear one of your asshole voices saying something along the lines of:

That's not such a big deal; how would that trick anyone?

or

I don't think I say any of these things to myself . . .

Don't fall for it! Begin listening to yourself over the next few days, focusing more on *how* you say things rather than *what* you're talking about. Slow your conversations down with others. Notice how often you or the person you're talking to uses these language tricks—such as the bolded words we've identified—to make their point. And in doing so, notice how they add a fine sheen of BS to the opinions being given.

Watch for how your inner assholes use these patterns constantly, taking simple situations and twisting them into huge f@#king unhelpful dramas of epic proportions. Running late for work perhaps? Instead of the voice in your head noting something like *Wow, I'm going to be a bit late today, that's not like me*, you subject yourself to something far more anxiety-producing like, *F#*k I'm a **loser**, I'm **always** late. The boss is **definitely** going to fire me!*

Let's identify, unpack, and consider alternatives to these hidden language patterns. I've even come up with an acronym to assist in remembering the 9 patterns. You're welcome . . .

The acronym is **G.A.P.S.** *of* **L.O.G.I.C.**, which stands for -

- Generalizing
- Awfulizing

or *a complete failure; beautiful* or *disgusting; love* or *hate,* etc.

Examples

- "You *always* have to have the last word."
- "They *never* listen to what I'm saying."
- "I'm such a *loser.*"
- "I'm a *failure.*"
- "I'm *always* running late."
- "I *never* get what I want."
- "What an *idiot.*"
- "I'm just so *lazy.*"
- "I *can't* handle it any longer."
- "I *can't* walk past cake without having some."
- "You *have to* get the vaccine."
- "I ate some cake; *my diet is ruined*" (followed by eating the whole cake)
- "I'd love to make it to your mother's place for dinner, but I *have to* go out with the guys on Friday night."

Never say Never . . .

"Always," "never," and all these versions of generalizing and labeling are **never** to be trusted. They are **never** (lol, see what I'm doing here) true. They are exaggerations designed to make matters seem clear-cut when they're simply not.

Admittedly, it's far more emotionally satisfying to shout nonsense like "You **never** listen to me" at your partner during an argument. Much more satisfying than the more accurate statement "I feel that *sometimes* you don't listen to me." I mean, it's hard to even imagine saying that last comment aggressively, right? It sounds like something you might say when you're trying to make up after a fight, when everyone has calmed down.

The problem with these generalizations is not only are they BS, but they also inflame and exaggerate the situation they're being used in. So instead of dealing with the real issue—why you didn't feel heard in this particular instance—the argument both escalates and bogs down as your partner points out all the times they *did* listen to you . . .

We use the same language internally, ensuring we put ourselves down in the most negative and demeaning ways possible. Guaranteeing we'll feel worse than necessary about our failings or weaknesses. Imagine, for instance, the unnecessary misery caused by telling yourself that *nobody understands.* This is an example of things people say to themselves that can seem to make sense at the time, reinforcing why they feel miserable. Yet there is a huge hole in the logic sitting at the core of this statement. And because of that hole, there is no clear path out of the problem. You're left with an exaggeration that makes you feel worse, while simultaneously keeping you in a loop of self-pity.

Let's consider the logic deficit that I'm referring to; the statement *nobody* understands. That's right. Not one person out of the 7 billion on the planet! No wonder you're miserable and that the problem seems insurmountable.

What if, instead, you got specific. If you were to ask your inner asshole some questions when it says things like this to you? Questions like *how do you know that **nobody** understands? Have you told anyone about the situation? Have you searched online to see if anyone else has experienced your issue? Oh, you don't have hands, asshole? Sure, let me type in a search for you then . . .*

Guess what happens when you Google "nobody understands me?" I'll tell you what - you'll get over 27 million hits on the search term. Hmm, I think you're not the first person to feel this way . . .

Or maybe you told some*one* your problem—that's *one person,* folks—and because they didn't understand, your inner asshole threw up its hands (I know, I know, we established it doesn't have hands, but roll with me for now), and is telling you, *see, nobody understands* . . . Now that's what I call an epic exaggeration. Jumping from one person to 7 billion in one swift move.

If you fall for throwaway lines from your inner asshole—like *nobody understands*—without challenging the BS it's serving up to you, you'll remain stuck in a problem that doesn't even make sense. You'll be unable to break out of the loop of despair. And not because the actual situation cannot be dealt with, but because it's presented so that there's zero possibility of really understanding, resolving, or moving past it.

Labels as the ultimate generalization

We all make mistakes at times. Sometimes we ignore advice or can't be bothered doing what we know is best. It happens to everyone. And other times we shine, we excel. We surprise ourselves and others with our behavior or outcomes.

The point is, folks, we are all multi-dimensional. We have our good side, our bad side, and everything in between. For instance, we can be excellent friends to some people some of the time, *and* real asses at others. We can be calm and loving parents, and at other times, completely lose our shit. We are not *one* thing, but many . . .

To label someone is to rob them of this depth and nuance—of the truth that they are rich and complex layer cakes—reducing them to the status of a single-dimensional cartoon villain.

Generalizations—made from a single incident, one argument or minor f@#k-up—create a state of permanence. For instance, rather than accepting our teenager may have f@#ked up in a particular situation, we get angry and tell them **they are a f@#k-up**. I've talked to friends and clients still trying to get over that type of labeling by a parent 20, 30, or 40 years later . . .

In the same way it labels others, the inner asshole also goes around labeling us regularly, treating us as *less than*. Reminding us with statements like *you're* **such an idiot** after making a mistake, diminishing and putting us down.

Like all negative labels, they generalize, they demean, and they are never the whole truth. They are *one* perspective at *one* point in time. Don't limit yourself to one BS perspective. When your inner asshole calls you names, spot the BS! Acknowledge that, yes, you made a mistake. Then recognize that does not have to translate into *F@#k, I'm an idiot*. Remind yourself it simply means you are someone who is growing and learning. And that mistakes are a part of the learning process. That, my friends, is a life-changing difference in perspective.

THE WAY TO deal with the cognitive distortion known as generalizing is to let the words become red flags. When you spot these generalizations, remind yourself that you are bull-shitting. Use them as a cue to slow down—to reassess the story you're telling yourself—and reflect honestly on what is being said. The story will never be as clear-cut or extreme as your inner asshole will make it out to be, and there will always be a more practical, realistic version of what is going on. One that is less harmful or hurtful to you than the version using these distortions.

Awfulizing

**What I convince myself will happen when I'm 2
minutes late for work . . .**

- You blow situations and issues out of all proportion,
  making problems larger than life.
- You make negative assumptions without any
  supporting proof.
- You assume others are reacting negatively towards you
  without knowing what they really think.
- You jump to conclusions, assuming things will turn out
  badly.
- You project minor problems into future catastrophes.

Examples

- "I made a mistake on my driving test. I'll *never get a
  license.*"
- "I can't get my head around this problem. I just know
  I'm going to fail math."

- "*They all hated my party.* They only came because there was nothing else to do."
- "I can't get the car started. I'm going to be late to work and *lose my job.*"
- "I just spilled my coffee. I'm such a *loser.*"
- Before a presentation, you tell yourself, *"I'm really going to blow this."*

As with generalizations, when we awfulize, we inflame and exaggerate the situation at hand. We are left with inflated problems that can never be solved, since they are neither real nor tangible.

Instead of breaking our problems down into manageable chunks, we create stories of epic proportions. *Everything is going to go wrong. I'm going to fail my course, lose my job, and my partner is going to leave me.* All because you woke up with a pimple on your forehead. Faced by minutiae, we present ourselves with epic dumpster fires and then complain about the heat.

Shoulding

- You often tell yourself what you *should* or *ought* to do.
- You place unreasonable demands and pressure on yourself by using unrealistic *shoulds*.
- Failing to live up to your unreasonable *should* statements leave you feeling disappointed.
- You hold on tightly to your *should* statements, creating guilt when you don't live up to them.
- When adverse events occur, you blame yourself afterward with various statements about what you *should* have done differently.

Examples

- "I *should* have a better job by now."
- "I s*hould* be up early exercising."
- "I *should* work harder."
- "I *should* be married by now."
- "I *should* be in control of my life."

- "I *should* have known not to go out with him."
- "I *should* have known not to trust them."

Shoulds tell us what to do, based on . . . well . . . nothing. It's rare to hear a *should* statement associated with actual data, facts, or any sort of supporting information. Instead, *shoulds* are used to deliver random stuff "convincingly."

"But darling, I really *should* go out with the guys on Friday night, I promised I would . . . " is a brilliant line to run when you want to hang out with the guys rather than spend time with your wife. But it's a hollow statement. Why specifically *should* you go? What would happen if you didn't? Would your friendship with the guys come undone? Or do you just want to avoid a more honest conversation with your wife? The one where you tell her that you *want* to go out with the guys instead of spending time with her?

Without facts or causes, these *should* statements often set you up with unrealistic expectations as well as the disappointment that comes when you don't meet them.

Other times, you convince yourself to take ill-conceived actions because your inner asshole says you *should*. That's not a reason, folks. An inner voice may tell you, for instance, "you *should* just do as you're told." But should you? Why? Says who? *Should* you just do as you're told, or would you be better off making your own decisions? I'm just saying . . .

Shoulds can be used to generate paralyzing guilt over what you *should* have done differently. People blame themselves for the shadiest behavior of others, telling themselves after being victimized that they *should* somehow have known better or done differently. It's horrible. The *shoulding* ends up magnifying the initial trauma of the event, trapping the victim in a cycle of shame and guilt.

Ly-ing Adverbs

Obviously I'd let you know if I wasn't happy...

- Any adverbs ending in "*ly*," e.g., clearly, obviously, definitely, mostly, apparently, really, absolutely, naturally, etc.
- These adverbs sneak opinions into a conversation as facts, or exaggerate the point being made.
- They can also exaggerate agreement without evidence, e.g., your friend tells you that Covid is a shadow government conspiracy to reduce the population by 90%, and you respond with "*absolutely!*" They in turn feel completely validated...

Examples

- *Obviously*, she no longer loves me. (Says who? Why? How do you know? Obvious to who?)
- It's *really* important to wear a mask (Where's the data on that? Saying "really" isn't evidence, it's just an attempt at making it sound more important)

- *Apparently*, Covid is a scam. (Apparent to who? Based on what info?)
- *Clearly*, you're upset right now. (How do you know? Can you read minds?)
- *Naturally*, I'm unhappy about it. (Why is that natural? Maybe you're just being over-sensitive . . .)

"Ly" adverbs—or "Lying Adverbs" if it helps you remember this category—are simply ways of making things seem *more* significant, *more* valid than they necessarily are. That's not to say they indicate lies, but they prove nothing and usually cover for a lack of solid evidence.

When you tell yourself, **obviously** *I couldn't help but get angry*, just remember, all you're doing with that statement is justifying getting angry without evidence or reflection on why it was necessary to do so.

Or when you tell yourself, *clearly, I was upset. Anybody would be under the circumstances* . . . Again, you are winding yourself up without giving reason as to why it's "clear" that you should be upset. Notice that statement also used one of our other cognitive distortions, *anybody*. How do you know that *anybody* would be upset in the same situation? I bet some people wouldn't be. Maybe spend some time finding out how they stay calm in the same situations . . .

Omission (of information)

- These are statements where information supporting the opinion being given is missing.
- They are stated as if we should simply accept the opinion without question, as if they were facts unto themselves.
- These are so common that we don't even recognize there is an underlying, unstated assumption.
- Usually, the unstated assumption hides a lack of evidence for the statement being made.
- Other times, the omission allows us to skip something we'd rather not admit or discuss.

Examples

- "It's not good to drink coffee." (Based on what data? According to who?)
- "*They* say you should eat more fiber." (Who are "they?" How do "they," know?)
- "It would be better to just end the relationship now" (Better for who? Better than what? Notice how this

hides the more uncomfortable comment from a partner, such as "It would be better *for me* if we ended the relationship.")

- "*Nobody understands.*" (Who exactly doesn't understand? Understand what?)
- "It's so hard" (Compared to what? What about it is hard?)
- "It's just not fair." (What exactly isn't fair? How do you know? Or is this opinion simply based on your sense of entitlement?)
- "I deserve better." (Better in what way? Better than who/what? Why do you deserve better?)
- "You can do better than that." (Better than what? How do you know? What research have you done to understand how much better can be done in this area?)
- "You can't wear that." (Based on what rules?)
- "They've done research that shows . . . " (Who are "they?" What research?)
- "Everyone says you should . . . " (Who exactly says it?)

Omissions occur dozens of times in most conversations. And there's nothing wrong with that, per se. They are a convenient shorthand, allowing conversations to flow quickly and comfortably in everyday situations.

But they should be a red flag on important issues, such as when someone is trying to convince us of something we disagree with. Or when our inner asshole is attacking us, based on a whole-lot-of-nothing. At these times, we need to be on the alert for so-called "facts" being presented as if they come from a legitimate source of authority.

For instance, someone tells us "*they* have proven the world is flat," with that look of certainty that only a flat-earther can seem to pull off without any hint of irony or doubt.

"No, no, *they've* shown the 5G network causes coronavirus," another person whispers with the seriousness of someone who has single-handedly uncovered a global conspiracy . . . working from their mother's basement.

Apart from being a red flag that we're hanging around with some real dumb-asses (I swear I just felt a reader slam their book shut), these are great examples of omission statements—important information that has gone MIA. We should immediately be wondering just who "*they*" are? Which "*they*" proved that coronavirus was caused by the 5G network? We are constantly subjected to all sorts of statements that sound legit, backed up by a mysterious "they." But just because the phrase "they've proven" or "they say" is thrown in, doesn't make it so.

Our inner asshole uses this approach as a tricky way of presenting opinions as facts, all the while seeming completely reasonable. It does this by using phrases that leave out significant bits of information. Information that would allow us to see more clearly the reality of any given situation. That would give us the necessary insight into the true nature of a problem. This way of talking leaves our issues tangible enough to feel the pain, yet abstract enough to make finding solutions impossible.

Always be on the lookout for omissions; the missing underlying information in statements of "fact" that are being used by your inner assholes to bring you down. After all, what would they really know? Most of the time, they're hiding in the dark.

General Negativity

- You can turn anything that happens into a negative.
- You filter out any positive news or outcomes.
- You reject positive experiences by insisting they "don't count" for some reason or another.
- In this way, you can maintain a negative belief even when it is contradicted by everyday experiences.

Examples

- You look adorable in a photo and receive many "likes." But your inner asshole reminds you that *it was just good lighting. You never look that good, really.*
- You do well in a project at work, but tell yourself *it was just an easier task than usual.*
- You train hard and win the event. But you tell yourself *it was just good luck.*

- You're given a promotion, but tell yourself *it just means more work and longer hours.*

General negativity is yet another cognitive distortion shown to be harmful. People under the spell of this distortion become caught up in a cycle of negative filtering that results in a poorer mood, which drives even more negative filtering. This pattern then spirals deeper over time, and can lead to episodes of depression, higher anxiety levels, and worsen the impact of panic disorders.[1,2]

Negative filtering can also be seen in perfectionists. These individuals often set themselves up for inevitable failure by creating unrealistic rules and expectations, leading to a cycle of self-criticism and blame. On the flip side, when they do occasionally achieve perfection, it does nothing to make them happy, as they "merely" reach their expectations. In this way, any possible happiness over good outcomes is filtered out, with plenty of opportunities left for feeling bad over the many failures sure to be experienced (or imagined).

Inventing Invisible Objects (nominalizations)

This is one of the most common yet least obvious cognitive distortions, infecting much of our language and thinking. The inner asshole limits our choices by turning changeable processes into static, conceptual (invisible) objects. Or, to get technical, turning verbs into nouns—hence the name for this cognitive distortion of "nominalizations." Doing so sends a deceptive message to our brains, hiding our involvement and responsibility for undesirable outcomes. If that all sounds a bit confusing, stick with me.

Take the following example: you sit with your relationship partner for that uncomfortable conversation. You know, the one where you tell them, hey, "we can't blame ourselves. It's not you, and it's not me. It's just our relationship that doesn't work."

Let's break this down. What you're effectively doing in this conversation is creating a third object—the "bad relationship." Rather than it being just you and your partner involved, there is now this third invisible "thing." You're taking the process of how you've been *relating* to each other (a verb) and turning it into a thing (noun) called a "relationship." By doing this, you're avoiding either person in the relationship from having to take responsibility for what has happened. Or the need for anyone to change their behaviors in future relationships. After all, it wasn't what either of you did. It was just an unhealthy "relationship."

What a load of crap! You can't blame an invisible, made-up abstraction—the "relationship"—for the problems between you and your partner. The actual issue is not the made-up object you've nominated as an unhealthy *relationship*. It's how one or both of you have used unhealthy ways of *relating* to each other. And unless you look at it this way, nothing will ever change. Instead, you'll bounce from one person to the next, wondering why you always end up in "bad relationships," rather than examining the pattern of how you *relate* to each new partner that leads you to the same crappy outcomes. It's how good or bad *your* relating skills are that lead to the so-called "bad relationship."

When someone says they think the relationship is unhealthy, a better choice—if they genuinely want things to change—is to shift the language from noun to verb; from the "invisible thing" to the actual process involved. So, the question might be something like, "how are we *relating* to each other in unhealthy ways?" This type of reasoning "unfreezes" the issues that are otherwise locked up within the nominalized verb, providing the opportunity for change and growth.

One way to look out for this type of cognitive distortion is to ask yourself, "can you put *it*—the object of the conversation—in a shopping trolley?" This is a reminder to ask yourself whether you are dealing with a real thing or an invented one, an abstraction or process versus an actual physical item. Can you put a relationship in a shopping trolley? No. Not a real thing then, so don't be fooled by the distortion.

Take another example: your partner tells you that "communication" is essential to them. Hmm, "communication . . . " Can you put it in a shopping trolley? Nope. So it's not an actual object. Try breaking it back down into a process and make the conversation about how they'd like you to *communicate* with them. In this way, you are unpacking the actual process needed to understand what your partner is looking for.

Let's try another example. Your partner tells you that "you never show me any *appreciation*." You argue around in circles for hours. They're sure you're an ass for even arguing about it. "You can't deny my feelings!" they shout. Meantime, you feel hurt because you're always doing things for them. But what if you turned their statement from the noun "*appreciation*," back into the underlying process of how they like people to *appreciate* them. How? Just ask.

"What can I do to show I *appreciate* you?" you ask, turning the noun (appreciation) back into the verb (appreciate). And maybe that's when they tell you it's not about the things you do, it's about how you speak to them; that they value words of affection over acts of kindness. Easy-peasy. Say nice things from now on and let them do their own chores. Win/win, right?!

To summarize, nominalizations freeze action in our brain and lock processes into unchangeable outcomes.

Turning them back into the underlying process creates the opportunity to learn, grow and change. We're back in the land of "the doing" and no longer dealing with intangible abstractions.

Remember, do the shopping trolley test. If it can't go in a shopping trolley, stop for a moment, and ask yourself, is it real or an abstraction? Is there an underlying process to explore and improve?

Examples

- "I've had it with all this *interference.*" Can you put *interference* in a shopping trolley? Nope. Not a real thing. So don't jump into an argument. Instead, start by getting curious. What do they mean? How are you *interfering*?
- Your inner asshole tells you, "You'll never find *happiness.*" Turn this back into a process. What do you do that makes you happy? What new things could you try?
- Your inner asshole tells you, "You're such an *idiot.*" Can you put an idiot in a shopping trolley? Well, ok, you can put a person in a trolley, but an "idiot" is a made-up concept. So, turn it back into a verb. Ask, "hey asshole, how am I *idiot-ing*? What am I doing? It's only this line of questioning that will uncover what needs to be worked on and changed. Otherwise, you're stuck with the static label, with nothing to do except feel bad or sad over being an idiot . . . without a shopping trolley . . .

Cause and Effect Reasoning (you/it makes me feel a certain way . . .)

- You often talk in terms of things that *"make"* you feel a certain way.
- You talk about feeling a certain way *"because"* a particular thing happened.
- You explain how you think or act in terms of *"if . . . then"* statements, e.g., *"if Michael is late* to work again, *I'm going to be so angry."*
- These ways of thinking reflect the cognitive distortion that something happening "out there" in the world *makes* you think or feel a certain way.
- This cognitive distortion style skips straight past *your* responsibility for *your* feelings and actions.
- It also means you will always feel like a victim, with your emotions at the whim of how others around you speak and act.

Examples

- "You make me angry when you get home late."
- "If you look at me again like that, I'm going to lose my shit."
- "Of course I'm angry. Did you see the mess he left behind?"
- "If share prices drop, I'll be devastated."
- "I can't concentrate with you looking over my shoulder."
- "The kids make me so angry when they don't listen to me."

We are always the "meaning makers" in any situation. Using Cause-and-Effect reasoning surrenders our power to the outside world of random people and things. Instead of deciding our response to events around us, we declare we are mere puppets without agency; doomed to having others pull our strings and choose our reactions for us as we make our way in this world. But we don't have to dance to the tune of others. Our responses are ours if we choose to own them.

Our challenge is to realize that any event can only impact us if it triggers something *inside us*. And we own the stuff inside us, right?

For instance, it's the inner asshole's belief that "children should be seen and not heard" that ultimately sees you lose your shit at the kids being noisy. Not the fact that they are loud (kids being noisy, hey, who'd have thought?). If your inner asshole doesn't carry the "kids should be seen and not heard" rule, you will not get angry. The kids won't *make* you mad because there's no rule inside *your* head to be violated. You only ever react based on what has been triggered *inside you*. No internal belief to be triggered = no reaction from you, regardless of the external event. Seriously.

There is enormous freedom to be had when you realize nothing can make you feel a certain way. That only *you* can choose to feel good, bad, or in-between. Now, if this statement is *making* you feel pissed because you think I'm talking nonsense (see what I did there), then you need to go back to the start of the chapter and begin again . . .

I get that it seems so damn obvious certain things make us feel a certain way. But remember, that's why this trick of the inner asshole is so effective. There is always something inside us, some internal programming being whispered to us by the inner asshole, that is causing our feelings. This programming, not the outside world, determines how good or bad we're feeling.

Let's break down a typical example, using the Cause-and-Effect reasoning "bad drivers make me angry." Now, is it really the "bad drivers" that make you angry? Or is it your expectation that everyone should drive according to your rules? If so, it's not bad drivers, but your irrational belief that everyone else should know your rules; should care about your rules; and should obey your rules. That's what makes you angry.

Now you might say "hang on a minute; it's not people breaking *my* rules that makes me angry. The government created the rules, and that's why people should follow them! I do, and so should everyone else. That's what makes me angry. All these stupid drivers aren't obeying the law, and I am. That's reasonable, right?!"

Maybe. Let's break that down too. Even if you think you're only getting mad because other people are breaking the official road rules, it's still not them making you angry. It's your belief that everyone should obey the law that's f@#king with your Zen. You need to ask yourself a few (more) questions:

- Do you really think that everyone is going to follow the law?
- If not, why are you still getting angry every time someone breaks a road rule? After all, people are simply acting as you expect them to.
- Do you really think it's your job to point out to people who break the rules that they are dumb shits who shouldn't be on the road?
- Did someone appoint you as the official "keeper" of the road rules and give you some sort of "punisher" role to go around yelling at everyone who breaks the rules? I doubt it.

If you're getting angry at other drivers, it's not them making you angry. It's all the patterns and asshole voices swirling around in your head about how you think people should behave. That's what's making you pissed. That others aren't following your beliefs about how the world works.

That's the sneaky part about this trick when used by the inner asshole. It honestly feels like it's someone or something else that's making you feel a certain way, which means nothing ever needs to change inside you. Because your asshole tells you it's not your fault. And because it's not your fault, you can't be blamed for getting angry, upset, or sad, every time something happens that you don't like.

But suppose you never change the dialog inside your head, or the beliefs about the world that create your inner turmoil. Guess what? Leaving that shit unchallenged puts you at the mercy of every dumb thing that happens around you for the rest of your life. As a friend once said to me, "either let go or be dragged."

Cognitive Distortions, a summary.

So now we've met cognitive distortions, using the acronym **G.A.P.S.** *of* **L.O.G.I.C.** , which stands for -

G.A.P.S. *of* **L.O.G.I.C.**, which stands for -

- Generalizing
- Awfulizing
- Personalizing
- Shoulding
- Lying adverbs
- Omissions
- General negativity
- Inventing invisible objects
- Cause and effect reasoning

Phew! Well done for making it this far! That was a lot to take in, but trust me there will be plenty of opportunities to practice. In and outside your head, every conversation is full of cognitive distortions, these G.A.P.S. of L.O.G.I.C.

The main take-away from this chapter is understanding that distortions provide a "back door" into your feeling brain, making everything seem *more* real, *more* important, or *more* alarming. These distortions are your inner asshole's sneaky way of infecting your mind with anxiety and fear.

To put this knowledge to work, start listening out for the types of language identified in G.A.P.S. of L.O.G.I.C. Get curious about what is missing. What is being assumed or not said? And then ask yourself the relevant questions. *Why? How do I know? What precisely is the problem?*

The first step on the road to change is awareness. You'll find after a while that you become used to spotting these patterns of B.S. They'll become small triggers of sanity as you spot the flaws in unhealthy comments and patterns. And as you question these distortions, you'll notice you are no longer bound by their deceptive chains of faulty reasoning. That you will no longer need to accept negative comments or beliefs as if they were the truth. Instead, you will become more balanced, more nuanced in your views. No longer pulled this way and that by the extremes of language sprouting from the average puckered asshole.

Mastering cognitive distortions is an essential step in managing our inner assholes. For that reason, we'll revisit these ideas with a clear process for managing them in Chapter 14, *Breaking the Asshole Cycle.*

References

1. Williams, L.M., Gatt, J.M., Schofield, P.R., Olivieri, G., Peduto, A., Gordon, E. (2009). 'Negativity bias' in risk for depression and anxiety: Brain–body fear circuitry correlates, 5-HTT-LPR and early life stress, *NeuroImage*, Vol. 47, (3), 804-814.

2. Allen, T.A., Carey B.E., McBride, C., Bagby, R.M., De Young, C.G., Quilty, L. (2017). Big Five aspects of personality interact to predict depression, *Journal of Personality*. 86 (4):714-725.

11

STORIES ASSHOLES TELL

It was written I should be loyal to the nightmare of my choice.

Joseph Conrad, *Heart of Darkness*

We've seen how our inner asshole comes in many flavors. Some prehistoric, driven by hardwired opinions built upon millions of years of evolution. Others, based on our own personal history. The voices of our past; parents and authority figures from our childhood telling us what we should and shouldn't do. Reminders of how we felt as a child when we were punished or victimized, ready now on a hair's trigger to regurgitate the same feelings and opinions when faced with hard times. There to remind us that we're still not "smart enough," "good enough" or "pretty enough."

Thanks, assholes.

In chapter ten, we saw how our inner assholes have a way of talking to us that confuses the truth about our true potential. They sell a story, hide facts, and twist the reality of what is going on around us, until misery and hopelessness seem like the only path available. Yet it's all BS. Every single one of the language patterns used by these assholes misrepresent the truth and drag us down in the process.

Now for the pinnacle of assholery. This chapter examines how our inner assholes get together for the big finale. The show-stopper where they take all their shitty opinions based on the past, all their tricky ways of spinning their fake news and mixing it into one overarching story. The Story of You.

This Story—or at least the part of it that limits or holds you back—is the narrative that your inner assholes have convinced you to take on board as a life script. Your role in this great adventure called life. It will frame your entire experience of the world. Do you really want the authors of your unique adventure to be the voices of fear and pain? Or is it time to turn that shit around? Are you walking around living your story or your life?

Story-making machines

Our minds are story-making machines. From the time our sense of self awakens, we seek to weave a meaningful thread through our experiences, organizing and making sense of our lives. These stories let us interpret our everyday experiences, making sense of puzzling or random events while justifying our opinions, decisions, and actions. They become a powerful, highly consistent source of self-persuasion and justification. Without realizing, we pick and choose our "facts," rearrange cause and effects, modify timelines, and weave them all back together to make meaning and give purpose to our struggles.

Sure, facts may be distorted, and inconvenient truths left out, but the power of a good story is just too crucial to our most profound need. The need for a life that makes sense of where we are and how we got here.

Who we choose to include in our Story and the way we choose to tell it not only reflects (and distorts) our past, but also shapes who we are and what we become. The end result—a story or narrative of our life—becomes an integral part of our identity as a person. The story no longer just tells us what happened but more importantly, interprets and declares *why* it matters; what it means for us; who we are, and what we will be in the future. It shapes our past, present, and *future*.

To tell a story is to take a stance

Some stories are provided by culture and society as "master narratives." Stories with themes like *stay in school*; *attend a good college*; *graduate*; *get a good job*; *marry and have kids*; and *then* you'll be a happy, well-adjusted member of society.

Other stories originate in the home. Tales told to you when you were small, that you took on as the truth; and through acting them out, made them so. Perhaps you became branded as the "middle child" and acted accordingly. Maybe you took on the constant comments from the family that you were the "smart one" or the "stable one," the "funny one," or even the "family idiot." The tipping point comes, however, when you adopt and begin telling this story as your own. It becomes the explanation or excuse for your behavior, with "hey, I never said I was the smart one!" as the comeback for every f@#kup.

Sometimes the story comes from watching others, the media, or pop culture. After seeing Wolverine or the Avengers go off to fight the good fight enough times as a child, you decide that your role is to fight for the cause of others. To be the one who saves people. To be the Hero. This can turn into a beautiful life, a version of you that fights for the rights of others when they need it most.

Or it can end up as a more twisted version. One where you find yourself drawn constantly into toxic relationships with people who need "rescuing," only to become their enabler. With you and the other-who-doesn't-want-saving, playing out their chosen roles. Over time, you start to feel taken advantage of, feeling frustrated and resentful. Meantime, because you are always there to solve their problems, the other person in the relationship never learns to deal with their own issues. Protected from the results and consequences of their behavior, they never need to truly change. Instead, they come to feel their own resentment at being "babied" by their rescuer. It's called a lose/lose situation . . .

Alternatively, maybe you watched your father taking crap all his life from family, friends, work colleagues, and bosses. You witness him shrink from every insult, never standing up for himself, finding refuge in alcohol, and just wanting to be "left the f@#k alone." And after watching this long enough, you decided one day that you were never going to be like that. That you would always stand up for yourself, no matter what.

Again, this may play out in any number of ways. An optimistic version seeing you become the most firm-but-fair person we all know; reasonable and polite to all, assertive but never aggressive. Or it could see you develop hypersensitivity to criticism, finding bullies where there are none. Constantly pushing back on people for every perceived slight or insult, as you prove that you'll never, ever be pushed around.

It doesn't matter how famous, talented, or rich we become. Until we shine a light on these stories that bind us, they'll continue to run their regressive patterns well past their use-by date. Take Hugh Jackman, a.k.a. Wolverine. Super talented, intelligent, buff as all hell, and an all-around gentleman. But also, someone who has been driven since childhood by a story of "not enough." Sparked by his mother—who abandoned the family when he was just eight years old—his story is wrapped around the belief "you've got to work really hard to make sure people don't leave." Driven by the decision to "make sure . . . that no one's going to want to leave me behind, ever," Hugh puts himself under incredible pressure to achieve perfection. That's a helluva lot for anyone to carry.[1]

Our stories spread and grow from these small yet potent seeds in childhood, tying us to our past, binding us to immaturity, trauma, and petty prejudices. Our stories take history and turn it into prophecy. What was, will always be . . .

We bend light and sound to the will of our stories.

Yet all our Stories are just that, *stories* pretending to be facts of life. But through their retelling, these stories take on a life of their own. They begin to run us, rather than the other way around. We end up like puppets, with our story pulling the strings. We confuse ourselves with our problems—with our story justifying why we keep getting the same crappy results.

Ironically, the fact that we are simply replaying a particular story while expecting the world around us to change, is often crystal clear to others—especially close friends and people who know us well. For instance, a work colleague once told me how depressed he was because his wife had left him. He explained he was sick of always ending up with women who broke his heart. Who wanted to run away after a few years.

"I've done everything for her," he complained, "and this is how she repays me. This is the fourth time now," he said through gritted teeth, "I'm never falling for this again! All women are the same. They suck you in and then take you for everything!" And I genuinely believe that he was so lost in this story that it seemed like the absolute truth to him. That he failed to see it for what it was; something he was co-creating, even choosing at an unconscious level.

After all, as heartbreaking and depressing as his story was, it was incredibly comforting at another level. By totally identifying with the story "I'm a nice guy that women take advantage of," it meant that he didn't have to take responsibility for always ending up with what he described as a "lying b@*ch that doesn't know what love is."

By making it all about his partners—by demonizing them, and then putting on the blinkers of anger and blame—he could protect himself from a far scarier truth about himself. A truth so evident to those who knew him well, having witnessed his pattern of behavior through four failed marriages. For it was absolutely no surprise to any of us who worked with him that each relationship ended in an acrimonious disaster. Why? Because he was a complete ass. He was rude, obnoxious, demeaning to others, quite likely a full-fledged narcissist. Yes, you, Dave. Our only surprise was how he'd managed each time to fake it long enough, at the beginning of each relationship, to be able to get them to say yes to his marriage proposals.

Here we see demonstrated both the positive and disastrous consequences of falling for our story. The positive part being that the story provides refuge. Safety. The safety that comes from knowing it's not our fault, that it's just an unfair world. That it's not us, it's them. But in doing so, we forgo the opportunity to ever learn from reality, from the truth—and in the process condemn ourselves to relive the same story over and over.

We miss the blindingly obvious fact that we are the single common denominator in every one of our failed relationships. I mean, for f@#k's sake folks, if four wives have left you in a row, and each time the same sort of behaviors, arguments, and outcomes have played out, surely you might start to see there's a pattern forming? A pattern involving how *you* form and handle your relationships?

And therein lies the rub. Most people would rather die for their story, no matter how much pain it brings them. Because the story provides comfort; it avoids the immediate and more challenging work of facing one's own involvement in the f@#kups we keep finding ourselves in.

When our stories become the armor we wear

Our stories can have enormous "protective" value for us. That's why it's so hard to let them go, even when they are choking the life out of our existence. Take the example of a colleague I worked with a few years ago, a woman who had grown up during the brutal conflict in Cambodia during the 1970s. The bloodshed and atrocities were as ruthless as any the world has ever seen. While she survived this brutality, she came away carrying a dominant story. One about the world being a dangerous, cruel place where she could only rely on herself.

Such beliefs left her feeling frightened and alone. But they also provided the strength she needed to cope with years of adversity as her country viciously tore itself apart. At the same time, they also left her with psychological defenses that would prove effective barriers to intimacy and relationships well into her future.

Living in Australia decades later, long after their initial cause had ended, these same beliefs saw her afraid of any unknown situation. Always trying to control her environment and avoiding close contact or relationships with others. Her story no longer served her, but she was unable to separate herself from that story. Because when we're in the middle of a story, it's invisible to us. It's the lens through which we see the world, leaving us blind to our role in creating that reality.

Performing a reality check on our stories

Reviewing the type of stories you tell yourself is one of the most essential exercises you can perform. Consciously re-examining how you've unknowingly arranged the plot points of your life to shape who you are.

Are they stories of bad things that happen to you? Are they about the government, your boss, or "the man" sticking it to you? About how others try to take advantage, how you're constantly mistreated compared to everybody else?

And where do these stories lead? Do they reinforce why there's no point in trying, that you can't help being stuck, downtrodden, or alone? Or is their narrative arc used to paint a picture of fighting back, overcoming adversity, and how you don't let other people be the "boss of you." Do you emerge stronger and more empowered from the stories, or as someone that recognizes and accepts their status as a victim?

So how do you perform a reality check on your situation? How do you know if it's all just a story that you should be letting go of?

Start by looking for recurring patterns. Always getting angry at others? Constantly arguing with your kids? Stray dogs walking up and biting you for no apparent reason? Perhaps it's time to examine *your behavior* and how that might be contributing to the problem.

Maybe it's your beliefs. Your inner asshole may have appointed you "Captain of the World" with the job of correcting everyone else's behaviors. Well, guess what, asshole? No one else cares about your self-appointed position as judge and jury of their attitude and behaviors. So, no wonder they tell you to go f@#k yourself when you give your opinion about what's wrong with *them*.

Here is a radical idea. Mind your f@#king business, calm down, and take a breath. Focus on what's going on in your life instead of trying to improve other people's "faults." Perhaps tell that to your inner asshole next time it pipes up with its self-righteous commentary that keeps you stuck in loops of anger and bad behavior.

Perhaps you're constantly arguing with the kids? Instead of blaming them, look for the pattern in *your* behavior. Sure, it's easier to just stick with your story about how kids show no respect these days. So long as you're happy to live in a toxic relationship with your kids, that is. Until one day, they put you in that nursing home, the bad one, with nothing left to fixate on but that growing lump on your neck.

Or, and just spit balling here, you could throw out the story you've always believed about kids and family arguments. Instead, you could slow down a little, breathe, and reflect on what you're doing to create arguments and change *that*. Because, whether you like it or not, it always takes more than one person to end up in a fight.

I don't even know you, but I'm willing to go out on a limb here and tell you that you're not f@#king innocent in these arguments! Maybe you flare up too quickly. Perhaps you operate on a "do as I say and not as I do" principle. Perhaps you think you should be allowed to shout, scream, and lose your shit at your kids whenever you want, but they should remain polite, calm, and even-tempered at all times.

Whatever delusion you're operating under, perhaps it's time to really look at yourself and how you contribute to the situation. I'm going to bet that if you do, you'll find things that you could change, and in so doing, your story *and your life* will change with you.

Let go or be dragged . . .

Your stories can be wrong about who you really are. Maybe it's time for an edit. To deliberately modify or walk away from some of them.

You can start this process by asking yourself a few basic yet powerful questions:

• What patterns seem to repeat themselves in my life?

• What underlying stories do I tell myself to explain these patterns?

• What role do I play in these stories?

• What stops me from changing the role I play?

• Who am I, if not my stories? Who could I be?

• If there is inner resistance or fear, which story is getting in the way?

Do you want to serve your stories or your soul? Maybe it's time to just let some of that shit go . . .

––––––––––––

References

1. Attia, P. (2021). Hugh Jackman: Reflections on acting, identity, personal transformation, and the significance of being Wolverine, *The Drive Podcast*, No.168, July.

12

NAZI ASSHOLES AND THE POWER OF CHOICE

Finding Choice in the midst of Hell

The concentration camp system of Nazi Germany. Delivering depravity and horror into the lives of ordinary people like you and I. Dragged from their homes without cause, hauled to the local railway station and shuttled off like cattle. Husbands, wives, parents, and children pulled apart, never to see each other again. Shoved, kicked, and beaten with rifle butts toward separate railcars on the whim of an officious prick in a crisp uniform with a clipboard. Your wife or husband, child, or elderly parents, taken in front of you as you watch helplessly. To be shipped off, beaten, and stripped naked, their bodies shaved by rough hands. To be herded into gas chambers for slaughter on arrival at the camps, used for slave labor, or sent for medical experimentation.

Dehumanizing, industrial scale torture and murder. A hideous stain on the consciousness of humanity.

Welcome to hell on earth.

One man dragged into this ghoulish shit-show was a thirty-something doctor by the name of Victor Frankl. Married for just nine months at the time of his arrest, he and his wife were deported to Theresienstadt concentration camp in 1942. His wife was worked to death, his mother and brother gassed. His father died of starvation and pneumonia. Frankl himself spent three years in four different camps, including the largest extermination center of them all, Auschwitz.

20 years earlier . . .

While studying for his MD and PhD at the university of Vienna during the mid-1920s, Frankl was concerned by the high number of teen suicides in Vienna. Despite still being a student himself, he began organizing youth counseling centers, recruiting a team of volunteer psychologists, physicians, and clergy, while convincing the city of Vienna to sponsor the program.

The free drop-in counseling sessions proved immensely successful, leading to a major reduction in youth suicide across the city. After graduation and gaining international recognition for the program, Frankl found himself invited to lecture at universities across Europe. Within a few years Frankl was appointed as head of the "Suicidals' Pavilion for Women" of the Steinhof Psychiatric Hospital in Vienna, seeing around 3000 patients per year.

By the time of his arrest and deportation, Frankl had spent over 20 years focused on helping others during their darkest hours, fighting depression, and preventing suicide.

The Camp Experience

Despite arriving in hell, it wasn't long before he was again trying to help those around him. Despite his own privations and unimaginable loss, Frankl worked to prevent suicide attempts among prisoners within the camps. Helping other inmates facing severe depression, he encouraged them to reflect on positive memories, scenes, and thoughts. And most importantly, to find their reason *why*, their purpose for living on despite the sheer horror of their everyday existence.

Frankl believed that while the Nazis could take their families, property, the very clothes from their backs, that they could not take everything. That there was one precious human freedom that could never be touched by the hands of evil.

The freedom to choose our attitude no matter what the circumstances. The freedom to choose our own way.

Coaching and counseling those around him, he would explain we are always free to choose how we think about the world around us, no matter how bad the circumstances. That when we can no longer change a situation, we must work to change ourselves.

He explained that between the stimuli of events around us, and our response to those stimuli, *there is a space.*

And in that space exists the power to choose our response.

And in the response we choose lies our growth and freedom.

He named this approach to treating people, Logotherapy. Today it is recognized as one of the scientifically based schools of psychotherapy by the American Medical Society, American Psychiatric Association, and the American Psychological Association.

And what became of our hero? Frankl was ultimately freed when his camp was liberated by Allied forces in 1945. Within months, he went on to write his most famous book, *Man's Search for Meaning,* dictating the entire work in just nine days. The book, detailing his psychological approach to surviving the horror of life in the camps, went on to sell over 10 million copies, and was listed in 1991 by The Library of Congress as one of the ten most influential books in America.

Appointed professor of neurology and psychiatry at the University of Vienna where he served until 1990, Frankl continued to write and lecture throughout his life. Along the way, he was to receive dozens of honorary degrees from universities around the world, while also serving as a visiting professor at many, including Harvard and Stanford.

Choice over habit . . .

Our inner assholes react to stimulus. Shit happens, and like hitting replay on a movie, the same stuff spews out of their mouths . . . err . . . asses? Think of it like stepping on the tail of a snake. It doesn't have the capacity for reason and reflection. It just lashes out in pure, instinctual reaction.

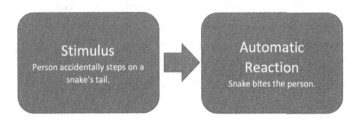

Unlike the snake, Frankl argued that to be fully human was to have the ability to turn our back on purely reflexive reactions to the shit-show around us. That instead, we have the choice to pause, reflect, and consciously create a gap between the stories of our inner assholes and our ultimate response.

To live out our potential, not act out our story.

Acting on "second thoughts"

The thoughts spilling out of our inner asshole create our feelings. But we don't have to let it be this way. It doesn't have to be this first thought—the purely reactive one spoken in malice by our inner asshole—that's left to drive our emotions. We can learn to separate ourselves from that first reaction, create space and reflect upon what has happened. Allowing our reflective thoughts—generated in the gap between stimulus and response, to influence our emotional response.

The practice of generating space for reflective thought can be as simple as the age-old approach of counting to 10. By consciously choosing to do this one simple thing, we are exercising the muscles of our *mindful self*—that part of ourselves that lives in the space between stimulus and response—allowing ourselves the time to reflect on what is driving our feelings, and perhaps choose another response.

Our entire personal growth challenge in life might be boiled down to this one task: the task of continuously, consciously creating space between stimulus and response and filling it with the tools that strengthen our *mindful self*.

We can grow this space through reading, meditating, reflecting, studying, and talking meaningfully to those who care. We can practice breathing, prayer, gratitude, and mindfulness; and by undertaking these tasks, fill the space with a rich array of choices. Choices that are ready to be called upon when faced with the challenges of daily life. So that instead of simply reacting, we reflect, select from our practiced choices, and respond deliberately.

Take, for instance, someone you know who is quick to anger. They have a tiny gap between stimulus and response. Someone simply looks at them "the wrong way" (stimulus) and they immediately get angry (their response). There's no gap between the two events.

Then take a person who has cultivated a wider gap, a greater space between stimulus and response. So, when someone looks at them "the wrong way," they don't simply (over)react. They don't listen to the inner asshole immediately calling them to fight or flight. Instead, they pause, reflect, and consciously choose their response. Perhaps realizing the situation has nothing to do with them, and everything to do with the person looking at them strangely. Maybe getting curious instead of angry. Asking the other person if they are ok? And meaning it. They exercise their freedom to choose a healthy response in any given situation.

This is the challenge for all of us; to recognize there is always a choice, and to then exercise it.

What will you choose?

We all have a choice to make. To live from our stories—the crap
our assholes feed us—or from our potential.

This book, at its heart, is an exercise in increasing your choices.
Arming you with the ability to mindfully choose your response
rather than being hooked in, minute to minute, by whatever
worry, fear or automatic negative thought seeks your attention.

The freedom to choose to live your best life.

Coming up, we will summarize the six key strategies our inner
assholes use to f@#k with us. Following that, the rest of Part 2
will give us the tools for overcoming each of these, and in so
doing, developing the skills of a world-class ass-whisperer.

PART II

TAMING ASSHOLES

13

YOU CAN'T SPELL ASSASSIN WITHOUT ASS

C.1620

The Shogun's Castle

Feudal Japan

The attack came in the dark of night. The ninja assassins were impossibly nimble as they scaled the walls of the stronghold, leaping silently from one foothold to the next across the face of the imposing granite wall. They had chosen this night for its heavy cloud cover, leaving them barely visible, appearing as nothing more than faint shadows flitting up and across the wall's surface. Having reached the top, the small team paused for a moment, scanning their surroundings, and then disappearing from view as they dropped noiselessly to the courtyard beyond.

Specialists in stealth, the assassins came dressed all in black, armed with knives and star-shaped throwing disks. Trained since childhood to infiltrate and kill the enemy wherever they felt safest, tonight's target was the most important in the land. The almighty Shogun, the supreme military leader of all Japan.

To be continued . . .

Are you ready to train, grasshopper?

We're going to learn to be the ninja assassins of the mind. Able to scale the seemingly impenetrable barriers of the psyche, kicking ass wherever we find it. Our inner assholes won't even see us coming.

No longer will it matter how long our inner dialog has been pushing us around. Ninja assassins don't care how well established or how well their enemy has dug in. It's time to climb the many walls that have been built to protect our fears and insecurities. To go to the heart of our nagging voices, the assholes within.

To do this, we need to know the enemy's methods. As Sun Tzu said in *The Art of War*, "Know thy asshole* and know yourself; in a hundred battles, you will never be defeated." To round out our knowledge of how assholes roll, we will unpack the 6 main strategies they use to f@#k with us. These are the strategies we will target with specific countermeasures in the remaining chapters of the book.

---

* MANY PEOPLE THINK that Sun Tzu said "Know thy enemy" in *The Art of War*. But we know better, right . . . ?

Six strategies of the inner asshole.

Asstrategy no.1

The ability to shape our beliefs through repetitive messages, a.k.a. nagging.

Many of our deepest beliefs and opinions are simply based on the messages we've seen and heard repeated throughout our lives, especially while growing up. These repeated messages are eventually adopted and repeated as our own. Or sometimes, especially for the rebellious types out there, the opposite message may be encoded as we seek to prove our parents wrong or to show the world we're "not like them."

Either way, simple repetition programs us. Be it through following the instructions of parents and society, or in our rebellion against them. This process is known by many names, such as conditioning or socialization, but we'll just call it *nagging.*

Yes, nagging works, at least in this context. The key to understanding this strategy is knowing that whatever can be built by nagging can also be overcome by the same behavior.

We will learn to nag our inner assholes into submission, choosing new messages to instill into our unconscious. While at the same time removing the repetition that drove the original (crappy) soundtrack of our inner asshole.

Asstrategy no.2

The power of exaggeration and personalization to get their messages to 'stick.'

Apart from playing on an endless loop, our negative assholes talk to us in ways that make them hard to ignore. They know how to get under our skin, to make it personal, to make it stick.

They exaggerate how bad or important everything is, blowing consequences out of proportion, and in doing so, making their messages hard to ignore or to forget.

We will learn how to dilute the exaggeration being used—by spotting and negating the cognitive distortions they rely on—and at the same time apply embellishment and personalization to messages of our choosing, ones that empower the voice of our *mindful self*.

Asstrategy no.3

They never get tired, able to keep nagging all night with their messages.

We've all had trouble getting to sleep at times. And one of the biggest challenges with getting to sleep can be the intrusive nature of our inner dialog. The A.N.T.s that start crawling around inside our brains. It's almost as if the inner voices are determined to turn sleep time into prime time for chatting, worrying, and muckraking through every mistake and regret we've ever made or had.

Seemingly never too tired to talk their shit, our inner assholes use this time—when we're tired and vulnerable to their ranting —to fill our heads with their stuff.

But we can flip this shit, and use the same process to load in new messages of our choosing when we go to bed at night. By substituting the tireless efforts of our inner assholes with guided meditations and sleep stories.

We can also learn several simple techniques that effectively 'gag' the inner asshole at night, preventing it from talking to us. Almost like flipping a switch, we can learn to turn off the nagging voices and drift peacefully off to sleep.

Asstrategy no.4

They sneak around in our head below the level of consciousness.

Another challenge in dealing with our inner asshole voices is they don't always speak their lies to our face. They talk their shit behind our back, chipping away at our confidence and peace of mind. So even when we're not specifically "saying" anything to ourselves, we might still feel an overall sense of dread or fear—sometimes manifesting as free-floating anxiety —without being able to pin down exactly what's making us feel this way. This can be the result of sneaky little inner assholes trash-talking behind our backs, out of sight, and leaving us to deal with the stinky feelings that bubble up like farts in a bathtub.

But that's ok, because we can use the same sneaky, out-of-sight, out-of-mind processes to generate good feelings too. Using hypnosis, we can set up some "automatic" voices that will keep running in the background, beneath conscious awareness. Voices that remind us how confident, successful, or happy we are, and let those feelings float into awareness at the appropriate time instead.

Asstrategy no.5

They control the media. Their communication network is wired deep within our brains.

As any good dictator knows, always take control of the media. Make sure yours is the only message getting out. Our inner assholes know this too, and they keep an iron grip on the voice channels of the mind. They pretty much own the brain's internal media network, our Default Mode Network (D.M.N.), which runs the self-focused chatter of the mind.

But as every revolutionary knows, if you disrupt this control of the media, you have every chance of setting a new agenda and changing the message.

And we can do just that. We can deliberately take the traditional media (our inner asshole voices) "offline," creating a window of opportunity—a chance to change the message. Several processes can be used to achieve this, creating what we will call a *transformational state*. While in a transformational state, the usual internal media network is downregulated, and we can load in new information or patterns.

Such states can be induced by processes that overload, wind back, or deliberately switch off the D.M.N. We'll review how to do this with various breathing methods, hypnotic states, and the curated use of therapeutic and ceremonial psychedelic practices.

Asstrategy no.6

They use emotion-laden talk and images to make their negative stories stick.

Adding emotion to any issue, topic, event, or discussion makes it more memorable, "stickier," so to speak. It automatically increases the chances of it becoming something that you can still remember twenty years later, for good or bad.

Taking advantage of this, our inner assholes use threatening and anxiety-inducing language, creating sticky patterns of thought and ensuring their negative stories become locked in. However, we can use this superpower too, making our chosen messages and stories stickier and more memorable. Using our imagination, we can tell ourselves emotionally powerful stories that drive positive thoughts, feelings, and behavior.

Knowing this sticky trick, we can also deliberately unpack the processes that make the inner asshole's stories sticky, removing or lessening their hold over us. We can also learn how to Teflon coat our minds, so their crap doesn't take hold or stick in the future.

Knocking the six asstrategies on their . . . asses

Having identified the six strategies of the inner asshole, it's time now to target these ass-clowns by learning the techniques of world-class ass-whisperers.

It's time for change. Are you ready, grasshopper?

14

BREAKING THE ASSHOLE CYCLE

Early 2000s

Johannesburg, South Africa.

A scene from my hotel window.

It was just another day for the homeless man living on the streets of Johannesburg, South Africa. As one of several hundred thousand people living in abject poverty in Joburg, he had no illusion of this day grinding out differently to any other as he pushed his shopping cart languidly in front of him. It contained all his worldly possessions. A couple of dirty blankets, a bucket, some extra clothing, and an old tarp. Plus some assorted items passersby would refer to as junk. But it was everything to him.

And so he pushed, ignoring the busy motorway to his left, just as the endless stream of commuters hurtling toward their very important deadlines ignored him. Coming to a halt at the congested intersection, he seemed to contemplate whether to make his way across, or to rest in the shade offered by the trees of the park he'd just traversed.

It was then he noticed the elephant, a star attraction of the circus that had pitched a tent in the middle of the park. It stood silently in the shade, watching the traffic pass by and the homeless man take a break, with what could pass as a bemused grin on its weathered, wrinkled face. The elephant was tethered by a rope that ran from its rear left leg to an iron stake driven into the ground. No matter that it could have pulled the stake out of the ground with about as much difficulty as you or I might pull the skin off of a rice pudding. For it had been trained to stay on the rope. A rope that today put it just within range of where the homeless man had stopped with his cart.

It was probably the sense of something moving toward him that had startled the homeless man into awareness of the impending encounter with his soon to be nemesis. Slowly but steadily, the elephant's trunk had reached out toward the man's cart, simultaneously grabbing and giving it a small pull.

And so the most unfairly paired tug-of-war match in the history of the world began. As soon as the elephant's trunk pulled on the cart, the man started pulling urgently in the opposite direction. This only seemed to increase the elephant's curiosity and desire to rein the cart in closer for inspection. The man pulled. The elephant didn't notice the man pulling. With heels digging into the ground and hands locking in a white-knuckled grip of the handle, both the cart and man were steadily pulled toward the elephant's large, curious eyes. Unwilling to concede the elephant's 10,000-pound advantage, the man continued to pull madly, even as he was dragged inexorably toward the elephant's face. This was a battle he was never going to win.

Arriving within a foot or so of the elephant's benign smile, both man and cart came to a sudden halt. Maybe it was the unexpected loss of the competition, or simply the proximity that he found himself in relation to this giant beast, but for some reason the man seemed to suddenly accept his fate. That his cart's future was not his to decide. The man's grip loosened as he stood motionless, watching with a defeated expression as the elephant rustled through the motley contents, gently moving items around the cart with its trunk as if being careful not to break anything. After a few moments of careful inspection, the elephant seemed satisfied. With that, it breathed out noisily, turned its head and went back to observing the passing traffic. Man and trolley were free to go.

Don't picture an elephant

Think about the story above. Did you create a "movie" in your mind as you read the story? Did you imagine an elephant in a park, having a tug-of-war with a man and his shopping trolley? Chances are you did. The words we use trigger images in our minds. And those images trigger our emotions. This cycle of meaning is how we commonly process the world around us.

Cast your mind back, for instance, to an argument you've had in the past with a family member. Try remembering who said what, and how the argument developed. Chances are that as a part of this recall, you "see" yourself in that argument, or some aspect of the other person involved—their angry expression or perhaps the sound of their voice. These images then trigger whatever emotion is associated with the original experience. Reflect on an argument for a while, and before you know it, you're fuming all over again, just as if you had been transported back to the original experience.

Our assholes hijack this cycle, using a vicious, reinforcing cycle of words, pictures, and emotions to grab and hold our attention.

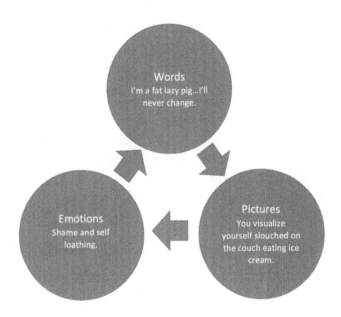

This chapter is about breaking the cycle of abuse by intervening at the "words" stage of the process. Identifying the triggers—the cognitive distortions used by our inner assholes—challenging their validity and swapping them out for something better.

Sticks and Stones

Words. *We* give them their power over us, and *we* can take it away.

First up, we need to spot the way our inner assholes use words against us. Let's say you're behind schedule on your way to a meeting. Sure, you might run late, but it's not enough for your inner timekeeper to simply remind you you're going to be a few minutes late.

Hell no, it's all up in your grill with "See, you're going to be f@#king late again, you'll be lucky if they don't fire you, idiot!" It gets *personal*—calling you an idiot—and *exaggerates* the magnitude of the problem—losing your job vs. being a few minutes late. No wonder we get freaked out and can't get the voice out of our head.

Exaggeration . . . personalization. Remember we met these villains in Chapter 10? These are some of the cognitive distortions we learned about. The BS our inner assholes use to get a hook into us, to make it near impossible to ignore their unwanted ramblings.

A key defense strategy against the impact of our inner assholes is our ability to identify cognitive distortions. And once spotted, to remind ourselves that they are never accurate—it's in the name folks—they are always *distortions*, nothing more. Lies and omissions made to frighten us. Because emotion gets attention.

So key number one to mastering words, pictures, and emotions is to *never fall for a cognitive distortion*. Instead, challenge it, getting to the truth behind it. Or allow it to float by without hooking you in.

Do this long enough, and your inner assholes will throw less of these distortions at you. Leading to a quieter, calmer mind. Milder pictures and less catastrophic emotions.

Challenging Distortions

The three steps to challenging cognitive distortions are to 1/ identify the actual distortion, 2/ challenge or release the distorted thinking, and 3/ replace with more reasonable beliefs and dialog.

STEP 1/ Identify

Get to know the cognitive distortions well enough for their appearance to become red flags in your mind. Their very presence as a part of your internal dialog should immediately alert you to incoming BS, to stuff that you don't have to take seriously.

Whenever you hear them, remember that you are bullshitting yourself. Use them as a reminder to slow down, reassess the story you're telling, and honestly reflect on what is being said. The story will never be as clear-cut or extreme as you're making out, and there will always be a more realistic version of what is going on. One that is less harmful, hurtful, or emotive than the version that uses these sorts of words.

Seek it out. And that journey, the seeking, will be a part of the healing.

The various distortions can be summarized with the acronym we met earlier, G.A.P.S. *of* L.O.G.I.C., which stands for -

- Generalizing
- Awfulizing
- Personalizing
- Shoulding
- Lying adverbs
- Omissions
- General negativity
- Inventing invisible items
- Cause and effect reasoning

If you're a bit foggy on what they were, go take another look at chapter 10. The more you get used to spotting these distortions, the easier it will be to develop a healthier relationship with your internal dialog and disempower your inner assholes.

STEP 2/ Challenge or Release

Once you identify a cognitive distortion rearing its ugly head, you can do one of two things. The simplest is to release it, just let that shit go. This is the art of mindfulness in real-time. Allowing yourself to notice thoughts as they arise, but not investing in them. Just letting them float by while keeping your focus on the now. On whatever is happening from one moment to the next without judgment or expectation.

Practicing mindfulness is an art that never gets old and is always a work in progress. We'll dig deeper into how to do this in Chapter 21. There's also a treasure trove of resources online for those wanting to practice mindfulness. Just Google, you guessed it, 'mindfulness.'

The alternative is to challenge the cognitive distortion as it appears. Challenge questions include -

- What evidence is there for this thought?
- How do I know?
- How can I test this assumption?
- Is this thought helpful?
- Am I taking things too personally?
- How else could I think about the situation?
- Am I blaming myself for things that are not my fault?
- Am I assuming the worst?
- What else contributed to the situation?

- Is this really a black and white situation? (Clue, nothing is.)
- Am I applying unrealistic standards to myself?
- Are there exceptions to the absolutes I'm telling myself, the "always, never, must" type rules I'm using?

For example, imagine you suspect your partner is deliberately hiding their texting activity from you. Instead of telling yourself *he won't let me see his text messages, he **must** be hiding something;* you could instead:

- Notice the distortion. The distortion is the "must" in the statement above. And then.
- Challenge the distortion. 'Must' statements try to trick you into believing something has to be a certain way, regardless of an absence of evidence.

Here, the challenge would be to ask questions of the inner asshole like, *how do you know he's hiding something? What evidence do you have? Is this a black-and-white situation? Where is this concern coming from, anyway? Is it because of your insecurities? Am I projecting a lack of trustworthiness onto someone else?* So many questions, so little evidence.

STEP 3/ Replace with more reasonable beliefs and dialog.

This third step is to overwrite the old scripts with something more useful. For instance, with the example above, you could move to an internal dialog of curiosity, asking yourself the question, *I wonder what's really happening here? Is my boyfriend avoiding letting me see his text messages?* No negative judgment. No assumption. Just curiosity. You would dig deeper into the facts and your feelings. *Do I know for sure that he won't let me see his messages? Or am I making assumptions? Have I thought about why it triggers the feelings I'm getting? Is it about his messaging habits or my last relationship when I was cheated on?* And after much reflection, if it still mattered, you could explain how you're feeling and have an open, honest conversation.

Practicing your bullshit-busting skills

The better you get at spotting and busting your inner BS, the better your life will become. This strategy has been one of the most powerful influences on my state of mind. I just don't get as wound up as I used to, because I can't help but laugh at the BS my inner assholes try to spin on me. Each cognitive distortion is an immediate trigger for me to scoff at their exaggerations and lies. Anyone can do it; it's just a matter of practice.

To that end, I'd highly recommend reading over chapter 10 again. Then for more resources, do a web search for "cognitive distortions." You'll find many materials, including worksheets, diaries, and all sorts of exercises to help you identify your most common cognitive distortions.

There are also some outstanding books on the topic if you want to read further. I'd recommend *Cognitive Behavioral Therapy for Dummies,* or *Mind Over Mood, Second Edition: Change How You Feel by Changing the Way You Think.* But there's a heap of books available. Just take a look and find something that suits your style.

Next up, we'll look at how to replace the crappy stories our inner assholes try to sell us with shiny new ones of our own choosing.

15

PUTTING WORDS IN ASSHOLES'... ERR... MOUTHS

Content Warning – this chapter contains references to self-harm, suicide, depression, and other mental health conditions.

2015
Sydney, Australia

Letter from a seminar participant.

HI DARRYL,

As I'm sure many people have done, I wanted to write to you to thank you for the seminar.

Making more money is not my point of interest.

Surviving my life is.

I have lived with clinical depression from the time I was quite young, and it is a battle that has, at times, taken me right to the edge.

I had adopted the honest opinion that depression is a war and that you either win or die trying. There is no middle ground, and even Robin Williams recently was verification in my mind that you can't grow old with this disease. I too had made peace recently with the fact (as has my mother) that it is in fact a war that I was losing.

Each drop into the darkness has become harder to climb out from, and every time I made it back to my feet, I was a little bit 'less.' Even when I would not be in a pit of depression, I have spent the majority of my life waking up each morning to a feeling of not being quite right or complete.

Although I'm sitting at work writing this, I am tearing up while writing. After your seminar the other day (having filled two notepads with notes from the day), I went home, re-read everything, and made some changes in my life to accommodate what I had learned. It has been a very fast shift, to say the least, but I am noticing a real difference.

Just days afterward, when I wake up, I genuinely smile.

*The only **affirmation** that I'm feeding my brain is, "I am happy and successful. My success in life is my happiness." I have made a journal of bright pictures which I've cut out and glued in, which is my definition of a happy and successful life, and I look at this several times a day.*

Because telling myself I am happy when I never really am is creating a huge amount of cognitive dissonance in me, my brain is working overtime to prove the new belief.

Everywhere I look now, I see something that makes me feel happy.

Thank you from the core of my being for saving my life.

Warmest regards,

Affirmations . . . driving changes in the brain

Before we go on, did you read the note from the seminar participant at the beginning of this chapter? If not, do not pass go. Go back and read it. Do it. Do it. Do it. Ok, hopefully I've succeeded in bending you to my will.

When reading the note (you've read it, right?) did you notice his comments about affirmations? How he used them to trigger a shift in what he saw and felt about the world.

Affirmations involve the use of deliberate, repetitive dialog—the same approach that our inner assholes use to harass us—but turning the talk from a source of torment into a superpower. We will essentially refashion our inner voices to lift us up rather than drag us down. We're going to keep repeating stuff to ourselves, but we'll make sure it's our mindful self that chooses the story.

These deliberately chosen repetitive thoughts—known as *affirmations*—are widely used in religious and spiritual practices, mindfulness techniques, and psychology. And before your eyes roll back in your head thinking I've gone all wu-wu on you, just remember we're about to go into the science supporting this approach.

Affirmations. Background, evidence, and efficacy.

---

affirmations

1. the act of affirming.

2. a statement repeated to oneself to imprint it onto the unconscious mind.

Affirmations have been around for thousands of years under different names. Many centuries ago, Buddhists started using them and called them mantras, chanting them repeatedly during prayer and meditation. Fast forward to the nineteenth century, and European psychologist and pharmacist Émile Coué, founder of The Lorraine Society of Applied Psychology, was pioneering affirmations in a process he called "conscious autosuggestion."

Treating thousands of clients from across the globe, he taught the use of mantra-like *self-suggestion*, another name for affirmations. He was the first to use the still popular affirmation, "every day, in every way, I'm getting better and better." His approach—known as the Coué method—was based on clients repeating this phrase to themselves routinely throughout the day, focusing particularly on the very beginning and end of the day. He understood that this could influence a change in the programming of the unconscious mind and its thoughts, which would affect our everyday emotions, reactions, and behaviors.

Self-Affirming in modern psychology.

You might recall we focused on the nonsense our inner assholes would have us believe back in Ch. 10 *Cognitive distortions. The Language of Assholes* and Ch.11 *Stories Assholes Tell.* Pushing back on this type of inner dialog and *replacing it with a better script* is core to one of the most effective therapies known to psychology today, Cognitive Behavioral Therapy or CBT for short.

CBT has become the predominant approach to psychological therapy in the US and Europe, with a large body of research supporting its claims, and a close alignment with the medical model. Long considered the gold standard in talk therapies, it is endorsed by the World Health Organization, the National Institute of Mental Health, and national psychiatric and psychological associations across the western world.

CBT works by coaching you to guide your brain through a different response process, gradually rewiring your brain's neural pathways in the direction guided by your mindful self.

Shown by peer-reviewed academic research to be as effective as medication, even for severe depression, a core component of CBT is to *change consistently and persistently what we tell ourselves*. Challenging the cognitive distortions we learned about in Chapter 10, followed by taking positive action that reinforces our new internal dialog.

Just how effective is CBT?

In a review published by Nature Reviews Neuroscience in 2009 titled "Cognitive therapy vs. medications for depression: Treatment outcomes and neural mechanisms," it was shown that cognitive therapy was as efficacious as antidepressant medications, and that its positive effects lasted longer after cessation of treatment.

Did you get that? Therapy that teaches you to change how you talk to yourself—reprogramming your inner dialog and then practicing positive action—was as effective and longer lasting than antidepressants. Their findings are not alone. Similar results have been found in countless studies, including the following:

" . . . *cognitive therapy patients showed a significantly greater improvement than the pharmacotherapy patients . . .* "

Rush AJ, Beck AT, Kovacs M, Hollon SD. Comparative efficacy of cognitive therapy and pharmacotherapy in the treatment of depressed outpatients. *Cognit Ther Res.* 1977;1:17–38.

. . .

"IN GENERAL PRACTICE, cognitive therapy was superior to drug treatment."

Blackburn IM, Bishop S, Glen AIM, Whalley LJ, Christie JE. The efficacy of cognitive therapy in depression: A treatment trial using cognitive therapy and pharmacotherapy, each alone and in combination. *Br J Psychiatry.* 1981;139:181–189.

"COGNITIVE THERAPY and pharmacotherapy did not differ in terms of symptomatic response . . . "

Hollon SD, et al. Cognitive therapy, pharmacotherapy and combined cognitive-pharmacotherapy in the treatment of depression. *Arch Gen Psychiatry.* 1992; 49:774–781.

"COGNITIVE-THERAPY PATIENTS SHOWED GREATER symptomatic improvement and a higher treatment-completion rate."

Kovacs M, Rush AT, Beck AT, Hollon SD. Depressed outpatients treated with cognitive therapy or pharmacotherapy: A one–year follow–up. *Arch Gen Psychiatry.* 1981; 38:33–39.

"THE NUMBER of individuals who relapsed at some point over the 2 years was significantly higher in the pharmacotherapy group than in either of the cognitive therapy groups."

Blackburn IM, Eunson KM, Bishop S. A two-year naturalistic follow up of depressed patients treated with cognitive therapy, pharmacotherapy and a combination of both. *J Affective Disorders.* 1986;10:67–75.

. . .

"Cognitive therapy can be as effective as medications for the initial treatment of moderate to severe major depression . . . "

DeRubeis RJ, et al. Cognitive therapy vs. medications in the treatment of moderate to severe depression. *Arch Gen Psychiatry.* 2005; 62:409–416.

These studies all point to the effectiveness of therapy that, to a large extent, focuses on challenging the stories our inner assholes tell us. Rewriting their scripts using a form of affirmation. Followed by reinforcing internal dialog with positive behaviors that reflect our new stories.

Yet how can this be possible? How does changing our self-talk possibly compete with prescription drugs when dealing with real biological conditions such as depression and anxiety? The answer to this question may surprise you. Namely, that talking therapy—with its influence on how we think and feel—leads to changes in the biology of our brain. Functional magnetic resonance imaging (fMRI) studies have shown that changing our inner dialog, beliefs, and behaviors leads to a rewiring of our brains, driving a virtuous cycle of thinking and feeling better. Leaving us with physically healthier brains.

Before we look at the evidence for this, a special note to anyone who might be suffering depression, anxiety, or any other mental health condition. These conditions are real, physical conditions. Please don't try to go it alone. Make sure you are getting help, ideally from a mental health professional. While the information in this book can be a useful resource, it may be extremely difficult to incorporate the concepts on your own, because the condition itself may interfere with your ability to think effectively.

Despite the focus for this discussion being the incredible difference our internal dialog can make, medication can also be an absolute godsend for some people. In fact, the data suggest that a combination of talk therapy and medication is sometimes a better choice than one treatment alone. If in doubt about any of these issues, please talk to a professional. You are not alone.

Changing our brain structure by talking back to the inner asshole.

---

*Science warning – this section is for those that want an expanded explanation of the research underpinning claims that CBT and affirmations can change the biology of the brain. If that's more than you need, or you're not a science nerd like me, just skip to the next sub-title, "Your brain can change. Just talk to it."

It used to be thought that the adult brain didn't particularly change, other than shrinkage and cortical thinning as a part of the aging process. However, in recent years, evidence has shown that brains of all ages can demonstrate both neuroplasticity and neurogenesis—neuroplasticity being the ability of the brain to rewire itself, forming new and different pathways or circuits, while neurogenesis is the growth of entirely new neurons.

Using fMRI and positron emission tomography (PET), images of the brain can be captured under varying circumstances. Such techniques can create a map of brain structures in individuals; as well as track brain function, including crosstalk and wiring between various brain regions.

In this way, over the last three decades researchers have been able to test the effect of interventions such as CBT on the brain.

Answering the question, does changing our internal dialog and our behavior impact brain structure?

Fascinatingly, CBT has been unequivocally shown to change the brain, explaining some of the positive impacts resulting from taming our inner assholes.

For instance, when faced with anxiety-inducing stimuli, research showed that both CBT and antidepressants led to similar reductions in activation of the brain's emotion center (the amygdala) in patients with social anxiety disorder.[1] In patients with obsessive-compulsive disorder, both CBT and SSRI treatment showed similar effects in dampening right caudate activity, a part of the brain linked to OCD. The decrease in activity in this part of the brain was correlated to clinical improvement of the patients in the study.[2]

Meanwhile, for patients with PTSD, a 2019 study[3] using fMRI patterns demonstrated CBT led to an increase in the synaptic connections between the bilateral superior medial frontal gyrus and right temporal pole, and a decrease in connections between the left cuneus and left temporal pole. These changes in brain connectivity were correlated with improvement in patients' scores on clinically administered PTSD measures.

Neuroimaging in patients with anxiety disorders has shown similar effects, with fMRI identifying changes to brain structures after CBT treatment.[4] Before treatment, phobic patients presented significantly activated dorsolateral prefrontal cortex and parahippocampal gyrus. After CBT treatment, these brain structures no longer showed significant activation when presented with phobic stimuli, suggesting fear extinction in the hippocampal and parahippocampal regions and reduction in the prefrontal cortex's dysfunctional and catastrophic thought patterns.

Your brain can change. Just talk to it.

There are countless studies using neuroimaging to demonstrate the incredible changes the brain can be talked into. I've mentioned just a few above. The brain shows remarkable plasticity in response to stimuli, physically changing its wiring and connectivity when faced with changes in our environment, including changes to patterns of internal dialog such as those used in CBT.[5]

Creating your Affirmations

Talking to your brain using affirmations. Here's how to do it:

- Pick one of the crappy things your inner asshole says to you. A negative belief that it whispers in your ear; perhaps a self-defeating story it repeats when you're feeling down.
- Now create an empowering alternative, an affirmation that counters the negative dialog. For instance, the negative thought *I'm such an idiot* after making a mistake, could be turned into *I'm always learning new things.*
- Keep your affirmations as short as possible - punchy and easy to remember is good.
- Start affirmations with "I" and "I am." In this way, you are mimicking the process your brain already uses for the things it believes about itself (think about how you explain your current attributes, either good or bad. They all start this way, e.g., *I'm not very good at math; I always get angry in traffic; I can't stand rude people,* etc.)
- Use the present tense. This is how we talk about those things we believe about ourselves, e.g., we say *I always*

get angry in traffic (present tense), not *I will get angry in traffic* (future tense).

- Describe what you want, not what you don't want. E.g., *I remain calm and loving when talking to my partner*, not *I will not get angry with my partner*. Using the negative version triggers imagery and emotions linked to the words "get angry with my partner" . . . they remind you of your arguments, not your good times. Remember, we want to rewire the brain so that our neural pathways lead us to good, not bad, patterns and memories.

- Repeat often and before you need it. Elite athletes train every day of the week, practicing how to throw, kick or pass. They wire up their automatic reactions to a ball being thrown their way before game day. They don't wait until the pressure of the game to practice their moves. So, for instance, don't wait until you're in the middle of an argument to start practicing your affirmation, *I stay calm and relaxed*.

These techniques are incredibly simple and yet so effective. The road they'll take you down, however, is equal parts fascinating, challenging and full of possibility. Creating a handful of affirmations and using them throughout the day; noticing and building on gradual changes in your perceptions and reactions; can bring powerful insights and unexpected changes for the better.

Why not pick one or two of your most damaging cognitive distortions, negative things you say about yourself, and start today?

References

1. Furmark, T., Tillfors, M., Marteinsdottir, I., Fischer, H., Pissiota, A., Langstrom, B., & Fredrikson, M. (2002). Common changes in cerebral blood flow in patients with social phobia treated with citalopram or cognitive-behavioral therapy. *Archives of General Psychiatry, 59*(5), 425–433).

2. Baxter Jr LR, Schwartz JM, Bergman KS, Szuba MP, Guze BH, Mazziotta JC *et al.* Caudate glucose metabolic rate changes with both drug and behavior therapy for obsessive-compulsive disorder. *Archives of General Psychiatry* 1992; 49: 681–689.

3. Santarnecchi E, Bossini L, Vatti G, Fagiolini A, La Porta P, Di Lorenzo G, Siracusano A, Rossi S, Rossi A. Psychological and Brain Connectivity Changes Following Trauma-Focused CBT and EMDR Treatment in Single-Episode PTSD Patients. Front Psychol. 2019 Feb 25;10:129.

4. Porto, Patricia & Oliveira, Leticia & Mari, Jair & Volchan, Eliane & Figueira, Ivan & Ventura, Paula. (2009). Does Cognitive Behavioral Therapy Change the Brain? A Systematic Review of Neuroimaging in Anxiety Disorders. The Journal of neuropsychiatry and clinical neurosciences. 21. 114-25.

5. Månsson, K., Salami, A., Frick, A. *et al.* Neuroplasticity in response to cognitive behavior therapy for social anxiety disorder. Translational Psychiatry 6, e727 (2016).

16

VISUALIZING ASSHOLES

Content Warning – this chapter contains references to self-harm, suicide, depression, and other mental health conditions.

E mma's Story

I was leading a seminar one time on how to supercharge the effect of affirmations by eliciting powerful, evocative images and emotions as a part of the process—similar to the psychological therapy known as *imagery rescripting*. The theory, I explained, was that using emotive imagery would drive change from deep within the unconscious mind. That their brains would respond to outcomes they visualized for themselves, no less so than in the way it responds to real events.

Now I get this might sound a bit "wu-wu." *Visualize what you want, and it will appear. Ooooh.* Accusations of "manifestation mumbo jumbo" and new age myths often came up around this stage of the seminar, especially with the more conservative corporate groups I encounter.

I was in the middle of just such a conversation with the participants when Emma spoke up. I remember it so well because we were at the stage of the seminar when I was expecting someone to tell me they don't get, for instance, how visualizing themselves staying calm or relaxed would change their usual stress response or simmering rage.

Yet that wasn't to be Emma's point. Emma, in her early twenties, asked if she could share an example of doing something like the process I was describing. Emma spoke of her suicide attempt at age 15 when she'd leaped off a bridge in her hometown. It was a bridge well known as a suicide location. Yet somehow, she'd lived. Despite extensive internal injuries and broken bones, she survived when most tragically did not.

Emma explained about a deep, aching feeling that had gnawed at her ever since she could remember. Of not being enough. Not smart enough, not pretty enough, not worthy of being loved or accepted. She had her reasons for feeling this way, ones we have all heard before. Treatment that no child deserves. It adds no value to repeat them here.

After recovering from the physical wounds of her attempted suicide, Emma started seeing a psychologist. They built trust and came up with a plan based around Imagery Rescripting, a therapeutic technique sometimes used within the context of Cognitive Behavioral Therapy. A crucial part of this plan was challenging and changing her negative internal dialog along with how she *saw* and *felt* herself behaving in various situations.

Part of her homework was to look into the mirror first thing each morning, and whenever she could throughout the day. To look herself in the eye and declare "I am worthy." To say it, feel it, see it. To visualize moving through her experiences, past and future, knowing she was worthy just the way she was. To see herself come through her challenging experiences, in ways that reflected her new image as a person worthy of acceptance and respect.

Emma explained that at first, doing the exercise felt ridiculous. "It was just stupid," she explained, but I trusted the therapist and had committed to doing it, even if it was "bullshit."

She described the first time in the mirror. Looking at herself, she stared into her own eyes and repeated slowly, "I am worthy." She noticed an immediate retort popping into her awareness. *No, no you are not,* it said. *This is just stupid,* it would interject. But Emma persisted. She looked in the mirror and kept repeating, overriding the other voices. "I am worthy. I am worthy. I am worthy." She visualized herself acting like a person who believed they were worthy. Worthy of love and respect, just the way they are.

For the first few days, she said the process seemed to remain about the same. Stupid. Various versions of telling herself "I am worthy," with other uninvited comments immediately circling in her mind as well . . . *This is stupid* or *why am I doing this,* all washing around with her new, positive refrain of "I am worthy."

And then she started to notice a difference. After a few days, maybe a week, she heard a new response. She had started her morning routine, telling herself in the mirror, "I am worthy," when a new comment popped into awareness. Something like *yeah, ok.* She almost jumped. It wasn't something she'd consciously willed; it just kind of came up by itself. Like so many of our voices, this one too was automatic and uninvited— remember automatic negative thoughts (A.N.T.'s) in chapter 4— except it was a more welcome version for a change.

And gradually, she noticed the change. Mixed in with her deliberate statement of "I am worthy" were other comments. It was like she had worn down the inner assholes. Having been outplayed and outlasted, it seemed they had decided they may as well get on board with the new story, if only grudgingly at first.

Now the conversation started sounding like "I am worthy," followed by *yeah, why not, sure. Yeah, I am worthy*. It was sticking. She began visualizing her interactions with others playing out differently from what had happened in the past, with her role as an equal participant rather than a victim.

After a few weeks, she had an incident with a family member that would usually trigger her feelings of "not enough." That was when she knew she was on to something. Because at the point where she felt triggered, instead of a spiral of "I'm shit" circling in her head, something different happened. With a will seemingly all its own, a different dialog popped into her head. A voice inside said, *"wait a minute, f@#k it, I am worthy just the way I am. This is their shit, not mine."*

And she didn't spiral. She felt like she could step back from the situation and realize she had choices. She no longer felt *to blame* for what was happening. She no longer thought it was her fault others were getting angry and projecting their shit onto her. She could separate herself from the situation, step back, reflect on what was happening, and know that being caught up in an unpleasant conversation didn't make her a bad person.

She said she felt like so many lightbulbs were going off in her head. She saw herself and the situation from a new perspective. Rather than finding herself stuck in a spiral of guilt and shame, she could "step out" of the situation and observe the reactions of herself and others dispassionately. While it was still a work in progress some 10 years later, she knew she had become a different person to the one that jumped from that bridge. Somewhere deep inside, she felt better, changed . . . worthy.

Nicely done Emma.

Imagery Rescripting

Just as unwanted, automatic negative thoughts generated by our inner assholes can plague us, we can also experience unwanted images and associated feelings. We might, for instance, find a particular picture of a time we were hurt—physically or emotionally—returning to haunt us. Other times it's a mental movie imagining future adverse outcomes—all manner of imagined disasters and things that could go wrong in our lives, tormenting us with their possibilities.

Imagery rescripting is an evidence-based treatment for dealing with these intrusive images. Just as we've seen that using affirmations can retrain our inner dialog, imagery rescripting can train the brain to flash up better pictures, triggering more positive stories and emotions.[1]

Mental images create powerful emotional and physiological reactions.[1] Research shows the brain will respond similarly to both actual or imagined images of events and circumstances.[2] Suck a lemon, and your mouth will be flooded with saliva. Imagine doing the same thing now. Go on, imagine that you've taken a slice of lemon and *put it on your tongue*. What happens? Can you feel the saliva being released into your mouth as you read these lines and *picture a slice of lemon on your tongue right now*? Our brain responds just as if there were a real slice of lemon in our mouth. In the same way, imagining changes to painful memories or possible future events can influence our brain, changing how we think, feel, and act, silencing our inner critic and triggering more positive stories and emotions.

The science behind imagery rescripting - visualizing the shit out of your inner asshole

Imagery rescripting and visualization techniques work by deliberately substituting bad memories with good ones. Or possible adverse future outcomes with positive ones—for instance, mentally rehearsing yourself remaining calm and confident in your upcoming job interview rather than stressing and imagining how hard it's going to be.

During therapy, patients can be coached in the techniques of 'imagery substitution,' replacing one image with another.[4] Specific painful images from the past can be swapped out for something more user-friendly. Or an entirely new image of a positive future or "best self" can be created from scratch, counteracting current negative internal dialog and images.[3] In a study by Grunert et al.,[5] 78% of participants experienced full recovery from PTSD symptoms after 1-3 sessions of imagery rescripting and reprocessing therapy. The technique has also been shown to treat major depressive disorder,[6,7] Social Anxiety Disorder,[8] and Obsessive-Compulsive Disorder.[9]

It's a poor sort of memory that only works backward.

Through the Looking-Glass, Lewis Carroll

There is no shortage of peer-reviewed, science-based evidence for the use of visualization to challenge and change our inner assholes' stories and associated mental pictures. But we needn't wait until we're diagnosed with a clinical condition. We can use these techniques anytime. We can reorganise the brain and drive new feelings and behaviors by switching out the inner asshole's critical dialog with alternative stories and images.

Using Words, Pictures, and Feelings.

Many of our inner asshole stories revolve around clear and compelling visual scenarios. The inner voice that keeps telling you "you're fat and lazy" triggers clear images in your head, of guess what, a fat and lazy you, sitting on the couch eating your emotions and anesthetizing your bad feelings with another gallon of soft drink and a pint of ice cream. In that picture, you look like a sad sack of soft-drink-guzzling, ice-cream-inhaling shit, and as a result, it's little wonder you feel so bad about yourself. Confronted with that image, you tell yourself things like "I'm never going to change . . . it's too hard . . . I always give up . . . what's the point anyway . . . " On and on, until you slip into a food-induced coma of despair in front of the television.

Powerful imagery like this drives negative inner asshole dialog, which triggers even more disturbing images and emotions, round and round in a vicious cycle.

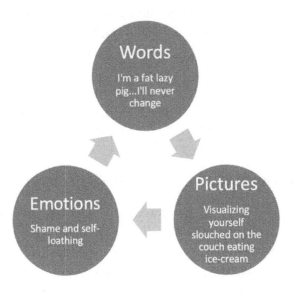

But we can use the same process to create powerful virtuous cycles too! We can deliberately use words, affirmations, and stories that trigger helpful and empowering images in our heads, in turn driving better stories.

The importance of a clear picture

You can only be what you can see. If you've never seen yourself as a walker; someone who deliberately takes the stairs instead of the lift, or who walks to the corner store rather than jumping in the car to go half a mile, then there's little for your mind's operating system, its collection of pictures and stories, to find as an example of what needs to change. People grow up reflecting what they see around them. Or rebelling against those images. Either way, we're driven by the images available as choices in our mind's eye, the stories and movies that inform our choices as human beings.

A key way that our mind knows what to do at any given moment is to dive into our library of images—recordings of who we are and what we know—and pick the appropriate response to what is happening. Suppose the image of a big greasy hamburger is the clearest, brightest, or most emotive image it finds as a response to the sudden thought *I'm hungry*. If that's the case, then that's the image that will drive our next move.

Our mind moves toward the clearest, brightest picture.

Suppose you don't like the available script or movie selection. Then it's up to you to load in the new pictures and stories you want and let them drive your behavior from the inside out. You could start small. Just picture yourself going for a walk whenever you're feeling down, rather than sitting on the couch. Tell yourself that it feels good to get outside and move. Remind yourself how much weight you'll lose by getting that exercise, and how much healthier you'll be.

That one new story and accompanying image, constantly reminding you to move a bit more, can make an enormous difference. Calculate the difference and add it to the story as you tell yourself about that image—the picture of you as someone who enjoys walking. For instance, that bit of extra movement means you might burn another 200 calories a day. Not much, you say? Just an extra 200 calories of activity a day is over 70,000 calories per year, equivalent to around 20 pounds of weight loss. Not bad for a bit of walking and taking the stairs!

Imagine that picture. You are 20 pounds lighter. Just by doing a bit of walking and taking the stairs. Easy to picture. Motivating. An exciting yet simple story to tell yourself that gets you off the couch and improves your life.

Just keep reminding yourself. Keep imagining it in your mind's eye. Keep sensing how good it would feel to take that walk. Don't try to make yourself do it. Your job is to work on the story, the images, and the feelings. Go for a walk when you feel like it. Because trust me, in the same way that making you think about yawning right now, picturing it, feeling it, can make you want to yawn—so thinking about, affirming, visualizing, and generating emotions will drive new ways of being. The new you, the one you choose rather than the one you accidentally became.

Adding emotions to our visualizations

Adding emotion to any issue, topic, event, or discussion makes it more memorable, "stickier" if you like. Add feeling to an idea, and you automatically increase the chances of it becoming something that you can still remember twenty years later, for good or bad.

Think, for instance, of those times in your past when someone you cared for, or whose opinion mattered to you, said something that had a powerful emotional impact. Maybe the first "I love you" from someone that you cared for. Perhaps an insult from or in front of others that put you down or embarrassed you. These are the comments that you can find yourself still replaying and stewing over, many years after they ceased to matter.

There are good evolutionary reasons the emotional content of our experiences leads to our brains laying down stronger memories—memories that trigger us in powerful ways based on their original emotional content. Unlike today, during our hunter-gatherer evolution, many things that might create an emotional reaction could also lead to severe injury or death. The roar of a lion, the smell of a forest fire, or the look of distrust on a stranger's face from another tribe could all lead to actual harm. The emotions of fear or anxiety they evoked ensured that they, along with any lessons associated with them, were not forgotten and would be readily recalled if triggered by similar situations in the future. An ancient part of the brain known as the amygdala boosts the recording of such memories, allowing for faster reactions, ones that bypass the usual cognition pathways when such memories are triggered and recalled.

Our inner assholes use alarming, anxiety-producing language. Language that triggers the same debilitating emotions as those the amygdala is programmed to detect and record as future threats. This means their stories become hardwired into our brains, ready for constant triggering and replay. One passing frown from a loved one and all the times we felt "not good enough" as a child can come flooding back into our heads, along with the inner dialog *I'm a bad person* ringing in our ears.

But if emotions can make things stick, we can also use this approach to our advantage. We can wrap our new positive affirmations and visualizations in a powerful cloak of invincibility by making them emotional on purpose. We can use our imagination to picture and feel all the positive outcomes that are possible. Making them "stick" more readily, overriding our old asshole voices that we no longer want to hear.

This process is easier than you may think. If you apply the steps above and really put yourself into your visualizations, imagining the whole sensory experience—what you see, hear, smell, taste, and feel all around you—then you will trigger the internal emotional response as well. Words trigger pictures. Pictures trigger emotion. The key is to let this emotion build. Notice it. Get curious about how it would feel in the particular situation you're visualizing. Expand those feelings, make them larger, stronger, more focused. For instance, if you're using a visualization designed to induce a state of happiness, then what does happiness feel like to you? Is it a "lightness" in your body? If so, imagine your happy state with your body becoming ten times lighter. Wrap your positive affirmations and images in this feeling each time you practice the process.

We can even use selective "negative emotions" to add to our visualizations that drive us. Take the example of one of the most famous basketball players to ever play the game. In the later stage of his career, he would psyche himself up using anger to drive a particular inner voice. As an "older" player (in his mid 30s), he would sit on the bench before getting in the game, repeating to himself the mantra, "they say you are too old . . . they say you are too old . . . they say you are too old," until his anger level rose to where he was bursting to hit the court and crush his opponents.

He used anger as a gift to fuel an inner voice that would drive him to take massive action for success. This is an example of carefully curating an emotionally charged inner voice that guides the desired outcome rather than a negative one. A more common example may be the "revenge diet" after a break-up, driving you to higher levels of health and fitness, just to show you-know-who what a mistake they made . . .

Visualizing the new you, today.

The techniques are not complicated. The key is consistency. Keep on picturing, picturing, and then picturing some more, the new you, until that image overtakes your old programming. You are rewiring and training your brain to respond as if the visualized image of a chosen mental or emotional state was already true for you in the present moment. Seeing yourself, for instance, remaining calm with certain people rather than getting bent out of shape.

Try any or all the following techniques to imprint new images for a new you.

1/ Visualize the outcome you want. See yourself succeeding at the behavior or goal that you want. See yourself hitting the gym and enjoying exercise. Picture remaining calm in traffic or hitting the ball perfectly during your weekly tennis game.

2/ Include as many senses as possible. Make your visualization as authentic as possible. What do you see, hear, and feel around you as you imagine the scenario? Keep adding details until it feels as if you are there right now, living the experience.

3/ Add emotion. Imagine how you will feel as you experience the image in real-time.

4/ Listen to guided visualization meditations. Just Google 'guided visualization'—there are literally thousands to choose from. They are ideal for putting your mind into a receptive state, readily absorbing images of the new you. Guided meditations combine powerful elements from the science of hypnosis with the proven efficacy of imagery rescripting.

5/ Create a vision board. Vision boards are a more tangible representation of your desired states or outcomes, typically a collage of photographs that remind you of your goals.

6/ Add positive affirmations to every visualization. Reframe your self-talk by associating a particular affirmation or statement that goes with each image. As you picture yourself smiling through a traffic jam, hear your mindful self repeating the affirmation that *I feel calm and relaxed, even under pressure.*

7/ Visualize regularly. The goal is to outlast and outplay your old recordings. Especially powerful times to practice your visualizations are when you fall asleep at night, and first wake up in the morning. Known as the hypnagogic state, this period between fully awake and fully asleep provides a window into a particularly malleable time for our brain. One hypothesis is that the brain routinely dismantles the mental models and constructs used to interpret our world as we transition through the hypnagogic state, creating a space no longer constrained by our filters and beliefs.

Thoughts can stray towards talking bears and flying cars without seeming in any way odd or remarkable, unless an unexpected noise or stimuli suddenly jolts us from our reverie; only then does our earnest conversation with a bear seem in any way odd or unusual. We can take full advantage of this willingness to accept any image as reality, by focusing on our visualization exercises as we fall asleep and upon waking each day.

8/ Make it easier to picture. Expose yourself to situations that make it easier to see your goals as if they were real. I've met many people who want to eat healthier, yet wait until they are hungry, to realize they don't even know what a healthy choice would look like. Let alone how to prepare or find it. What chance do they have of achieving healthy eating? It's hard to visualize what you have never seen or done. No wonder they slide back to the images already in their mind - of how to make mac-and-cheese instead . . . we move toward the clearest, brightest pictures.

References

1. Gerrards-Hesse A., Spies K., Hesse F. W. (1994). Experimental inductions of emotional states and their effectiveness: A review. Br J Psychol, 85(1), 55–78.

2. Skottnik, L., Linden, D. (2019). Mental Imagery and Brain Regulation—New Links Between Psychotherapy and Neuroscience. Frontiers in Psychiatry, 10, 779.

3. Van Der Kolk, B. A., Van Der Hart, O. (1989). Pierre Janet and the breakdown of adaptation in psychological trauma. American Journal of Psychiatry, 146, 1530–1540.

4. Holmes EA, Arntz A, Smucker M. R. Imagery rescripting in cognitive behaviour therapy: images, treatment techniques and outcomes. J Behav Ther Exp Psychiatry. 2007 Dec; 38(4):297-305.

5. Grunert, B. K., Weis, J. M., Smucker, M. R., & Christianson, H. (2007). Imagery rescripting and reprocessing therapy after failed prolonged imaginal exposure for posttraumatic stress

disorder following industrial injury. Journal of Behaviour Therapy and Experimental Psychiatry.

6. Brewin CR, Wheatley J, Patel T, Fearon P, Hackmann A, Wells A, Fisher P, Myers S. Imagery rescripting as a brief stand-alone treatment for depressed patients with intrusive memories. Behav Res Ther. 2009 Jul; 47(7):569-76.

7. Wheatley, J., Brewin, C. R., Patel, T., Hackmann, E. A., Wells, A., Fisher, P., Myers, S. (2007). "I'll believe it when I can see it": imagery rescripting of intrusive sensory memories in depression. Journal of Behavior Therapy and Experimental Psychiatry, 38, 371–385

8. Norton, A. R., Abbott, M. J. (2016). The efficacy of imagery rescripting compared to cognitive restructuring for social anxiety disorder, Journal of Anxiety Disorders, 40, 18-28

9. Morina, N., Lancee, J., Arntz, A. (2017). Imagery rescripting as a clinical intervention for aversive memories: A meta-analysis, Journal of Behavior Therapy and Experimental Psychiatry, 55, 6-15

17

SUFFOCATING ASSHOLES

"Breathe Motherfucker"

Wim Hof

It was a beautiful sunny day on the outskirts of Amsterdam, The Netherlands, and I was taking part in my very first breathwork session. The session was part of a 3-day retreat focused on the use of psychedelic plant medicine and altered states of consciousness, run in conjunction with a study out of Imperial College London on the effects of psychedelics on enhancing creativity.

As an active researcher and writer about transformational states, I was excited to be a part of the program. The bonus was that as an attendee at the workshop, I was to receive a high dose psychedelic experience, contributing to the research whilst also exploring how psychedelics might expand my creativity as a writer. I'll let you be the judge . . .

As a prelude to the upcoming psychedelic experience, our group had been offered the opportunity to try out something called breathwork. I figured why not? After all, a little breathing seemed simple enough. I mean, I'd been doing it my whole life right, so what could possibly go wrong?

The session facilitator was Sven Kimenai.* Sven, with qualifications in psychobiology and extensive experience in leading breathwork, cold therapy, meditation, and psychedelic transformational processes, started by explaining how the session would unfold. He would be guiding us in a pattern of deeper and faster-than-usual breathing, with no pause between inhale and exhale. Powerful music would be accompanied by occasional invitations to shake parts of our bodies or make various noises and chants. It all sounded a bit new age and flaky. Still, I'd promised myself to "lean into" new experiences on this retreat, so I decided to give it everything I could.

Meantime, Sven explained some of the sensations we might experience so as not to alarm us during the session. These included the possibility of light dizziness, tingling in our hands and feet, uncontrolled spasms, laughter or tears, and wait for it, "lobster claws." Apparently, we might feel our hands becoming inexplicably clenched up like, well, lobster claws. Hmm, ok, it really was sounding flaky, but again I was keen to give it a shot.

Breathwork - a little background . . .

Breathwork has its roots in traditional healing and mystic practices that have been around for thousands of years. For instance, Pranayama, still practiced today, is thought to have originated around the fifth century BCE and is mentioned in early yogic texts such as the Bhagavad Gita. Qigong is another breath practice that originated around 4,000 years ago and is still widely used today.

In its modern form, breathwork is a generic term for various breathing practices that focus on conscious control of breathing, generally for improving health, relaxing, and generating altered states of consciousness.

Two branches of Breath Practice

For the purposes of managing our inner asshole, we can break breathwork into two distinct approaches. Think of one approach as being **"slow and calm,"** and the other as **"fast and intense."** Both have valuable applications in managing our inner asshole, and we'll look at each separately, beginning with "slow and calm."

Type 1 - Slow and calm breathing.

Slow and calm breathing covers a range of techniques focused on relaxing the mind. We can use these methods at any time when stress or anxiety threatens us. Designed to calm the body and mind, they are straightforward to learn and use, and work almost instantly. And they are practical and powerful enough to have been adopted by hospitals, police departments, military, and other first responders to help them stay focused, calm, and resourceful.

These slow and calming styles of breathwork also represent the most accessible avenue into effective meditation for most people, reducing the activity of the default mode network—the brain region behind our inner asshole voices.

By deliberately controlling our breath, we can interrupt habits and patterns that prevent us from living and performing at our best. Our rate and style of breath hacks directly into our stress systems, calming our body, mind, and self-talk.

While there are many brands and schools suggesting very particular approaches to this type of calm and deliberate breathing, they all entail the same general approach: *Slowing the breath down to around 5 to 6 breaths per minute for a few minutes while breathing diaphragmatically—from deep in the belly rather than up high in the chest.*

That's largely it.

But don't be fooled. Despite its simplicity, this practice of deliberately slowing the breath taps into a full suite of physiological processes that will calm your mind and body, reduce heart rate and blood pressure, relax your muscles, and increase feelings of peacefulness.

The Science of Slow and Calm Breathing

Our heart rate, blood pressure, digestive system, stress response and rate of breath are all managed without conscious control or awareness by our autonomic nervous system. This system responds to our environment, continuously tweaking body functions in response to internal and external stimuli.

For instance, when faced with stressful stimuli, our autonomic nervous system might be triggered into a fight-or-flight response. Adrenaline is released into our bloodstream, leading to shallow breathing, faster heart rate, increased blood pressure and sugar metabolism. Blood is redirected from such activity as digestion toward the large muscle groups, ready for fight or flight.

However, through consciously choosing our breath rate and style, we can tap directly into the autonomic nervous system, deliberately influencing our physiological and psychological settings. We can turn down the dial from stressed to calm, *soothing the inner asshole voices at the same time.*[4] This incredibly simple choice—of how we breathe—regulates the autonomic nervous system, calming the mind and reversing the settings described above. The body is returned to the "rest and digest" state by a few minutes of mindful breath.[1]

Neuroimaging research has shown these breathing techniques to influence parts of the brain involved in managing thoughts, moods, and experiences.[2] By bringing ourselves back to "center," becoming mindful of our breath and turning off the fight-or-flight response, we also calm the inner asshole.[3] These simple, slow breathing exercises have been shown to lead to increased activity in cortical and subcortical brain structures, which relate to increased relaxation, reduced anxiety, depression and anger.[4]

Time to try

We're going to learn two popular approaches you can try right now. Both techniques (along with most conscious breathing practices) involve a shift from our usual high-in-the-chest style of breathing to deeper, diaphragmatic breathing, sometimes known as belly breathing. So, let's quickly learn about belly breathing, and then we'll apply it to the two techniques; box breathing and the 4-7-8 technique .

Belly Breathing

As we become stressed, our breathing shifts up into the chest. To inflate the lungs, we lift the rib cage up and outwards. Think of a panting dog. We don't want to be panting like a dog, right? Instead, we want to use our diaphragm, breathing from deeper down in the lower rib cage, rather than higher in our chest. This is what we mean by belly breathing.

To picture what this looks like, think of a baby sleeping on its back. Babies are natural belly breathers. As they sleep, we can see their belly rising up and down with each inhale and exhale. They're relaxed. Sleeping like, well, a baby.

Try it now. Place your right hand on your chest and your left hand on your belly and then breathe by pushing in and out with the belly. You should be able to do it without feeling any movement of your right hand.

Ok, so that's diaphragmatic or belly breathing. Now for those two slow breathing techniques that you can apply anytime to calm your inner asshole.

Breathing like a SEAL - Box breathing.

Navy SEALs might come under a little pressure from time to time . . . right? One way they are taught to stay calm is through this incredibly simple breathing technique. Called Box breathing, it works like this -

- Get comfortable. Sitting or lying down is fine.
- Remember to breathe diaphragmatically. Do this by pushing your belly outward on the in-breath to inflate your lungs.
- Start with an inhale of 4 seconds through the nose.
- Hold for 4 seconds (while your lungs are inflated).
- Exhale for 4 seconds through the nose.
- Hold for 4 seconds (while your lungs are empty).
- And repeat . . .

That was one breath cycle. Keep doing this for 5 minutes or until feeling relaxed.

4-7-8 Breathing

The 4-7-8 breathing technique, also known as Relaxing Breath, is a technique developed by a pioneer and leader in integrative medicine, Dr. Andrew Weil. Dr. Weil describes this technique as a "natural tranquilizer for the nervous system," reducing stress and helping you fall asleep within minutes.

It goes like this -

- Keep the tip of your tongue up against the gum tissue just above the back of your front teeth.
- Breathe out through the mouth with a whooshing sound.
- Close the mouth and inhale softly through the nose for a count of 4.
- Hold for a count of 7.
- Exhale using the mouth with a whooshing sound for a count of 8.

That was one breath cycle. The time spent doing the cycle is not particularly important as long as you keep the 4, 7, 8 ratio constant.

Dr. Weil suggests starting with no more than 4 cycles for the first few weeks of practice. Be aware you may feel a little light-headed when you first use the technique, but this too will pass. He suggests doing the technique at least twice a day, and more often as required to reduce stress at any time. Its effects improve with practice, so stick with it for a few weeks to see maximum results!

For anyone interested in taking a deeper dive into all things related to a healthy lifestyle, I recommend looking at his website, drweil.com, or one of his many books on health and lifestyle. He also has some great explanations and video demonstrations on how to do the 4-7-8 breathing technique on the site.

A quick online search for "breathe to reduce stress" will uncover plenty of research, articles, and video demonstrations on these and other techniques.

Type 2 - Fast and intense breath practices

The second approach to breathwork—Fast and Intense— revolves around intensive breathing practices designed to create peak experiences. Often profound in their effect, these techniques are not for general everyday situations. The instruction on some medicines of "do not use while driving or operating heavy machinery" comes to mind.

Instead, participation in such practices often takes place as a part of specialized workshops and retreats, as a psychological and emotional circuit breaker or intervention. They reliably induce altered states that can be harnessed to reset the mind, loosening old habits of thought and behavior. Participants often describe such practices as feeling like twenty years of therapy in a day.

The modern development of Fast and Intense breathwork for altering states of consciousness

The modern development of breathwork for altering states of consciousness was born out of the altogether different, yet in some ways related, realm of psychedelic medicines. Research during the 1950s and 60s was proving such medicines highly effective in treating those with a range of psychological conditions, along with those seeking growth and transformation.

But then the US Congress enacted the Controlled Substances Act in 1970, placing hallucinogenic drugs into Schedule 1—the category reserved for those considered most dangerous and with no medical benefit—bringing research and its funding to a screaming halt virtually overnight.

Many psychotherapists gave up on researching psychedelic compounds and transformational states at that point. However, a psychiatrist named Stanislav Grof was not to be deterred. At the time, Grof was a clinical and research Fellow at the Henry Phipps Clinic, part of the Johns Hopkins University School of Medicine in Baltimore. By the stage these new restrictions were passed he had already spent years studying the effects of LSD; its impact on altered states of consciousness; along with how it could be used in psycho-spiritual healing and growth.

Joined by his wife Christina Grof MD, they searched for alternative legal methods of inducing such altered states, ultimately developing an approach based on fast and intense breathing in the early 70s. They named this approach Holotropic Breathwork after the Greek words *holos*, meaning *whole*, and *trepein*, meaning *to move toward*. Moving toward wholeness.

They found their breathing techniques allowed people to reach fully hallucinogenic states without the use of banned substances. Others in the fields of psychology and psychospiritual development started developing similar practices around the same time, with similar results.

Wait a minute. Did you catch what I just said? I think we should give it a moment to really sink in . . . They found their breathing techniques allowed people to reach fully hallucinogenic states without the use of banned substances.

Getting high. Tripping. No drugs, just breathing . . .

My Amsterdam Breathwork Session cont.

The group settled in on their yoga mats. We were lying comfortably on our backs, listening to relaxing music and Sven's reassuring instructions. I adjusted my eye mask, plunging me into complete darkness as the music and Sven's voice washed around us.

I thought to myself that at least with the blindfolds on, nobody would see what I looked like if I developed these so-called "lobster claws," right? Not to mention all the promised gnashing of teeth, writhing and weeping like a small child! Anonymity assured, I was even more determined to lean into the experience and see if I could reach a psychedelic state without the drugs.

As the session started, Sven led us through a deeper, faster breathing pattern than normal. Meanwhile, the music was wrenched up loud. Emotive, evocative music that challenged us to keep up and to reach within, triggering internal reactions like only music can.

Now and then we'd be called on to give our bodies a shake, to flail our limbs or to release whatever guttural noise seemed fit to release from deep within. Sounds kooky, right? But leaning in, I found myself caught up in something.

Within just a few brief minutes, I noticed my arms and legs were tingling strangely. My face too. Then came the lobster claws. My hands and fingers scrunching up, tightening into the shape of strange little hooves or claws. By now, my whole body felt like it had an agenda of its own, and I was simply along for the ride.

Tears started rolling down my cheeks. A trickle became a flood. I did not know why. I wasn't upset; in fact, I felt waves of gratitude and love wash over me, seemingly through every cell of my body. This was interspersed with a profound sense of calm. Somewhere amongst all that, I also remember feeling like I was floating just outside my body. Yet I felt incredibly present all at the same time.

And so it continued. I wept uncontrollably, thrashed around like a fish on the end of a line, tingled, and clawed the air, all the while feeling strangely at one with the music. Then it was over. It felt like we'd been at it for about 15 minutes. It had been over an hour.

I laid back, feeling physically exhausted in an entirely wonderful way. I felt more connected to my body than I could remember having ever been, and my mind and emotions were in a state of elated calm. Strange indeed, my friends, strange indeed.

Yet stranger things were still to come. I've had tightness in my middle back for about ten years. I have tried everything over time, from physiotherapy, chiropathy, cupping, remedial massage, acupuncture, you name it. Most things helped a little, but I was used to it being there, a nagging but not debilitating tightness and discomfort that I'd learned to put up with.

It was gone. The pain in my middle back had disappeared. How, I wondered? No mention had been made of possible pain relief at the introduction to the session by Sven, so it couldn't have been a placebo effect. Talking to him after the session, he explained that participants often spoke of finding relief from chronic pain after undertaking breathwork. From his explanation, and what I could find during later research, the deep relaxation induced during breathwork can break the cycle of tense muscles impacting surrounding nerves, easing tension around chronic pain sites. It is also hypothesized that breathwork leads to release of endogenous opioids. Higher levels of endogenous opioids would also enhance muscle relaxation, as well as improving pain threshold.

Beyond the unexpected pain relief, the breathwork session left me feeling calm and connected. Like the warm afterglow of some chemically induced high, I felt completely chilled out, mellow, centered. There was also a powerful sense of the cathartic about it, like I'd received an emotional enema via a firehose. I felt lighter, like I was floating through my experiences and interactions with others over the next few days. Incredible! Who'd have thought heavy breathing could ever be associated with such a good time . . .

This strange state of mind is what I referred to earlier as a *transformational state*. And we want to go there because this state of mind is the space where change is made possible. Our inner dialog quietens down. We are more open to new options, new ideas. And we give the unconscious mind the space and opportunity to do a little rewiring.[6]

How Fast Intense Breathwork works . . .

So why had I felt so strange after the breathwork session? What had happened to me?

Branded versions of breathwork come in all shapes and flavors. Because of its powerful effects, many practitioners have wrapped the process tightly in their various belief systems and particular styles of personal development and healing.

Some claim that its effects result from opening your chakras and improving the flow of chi around your body. Others claim the effects are a result of increasing your level of universal life force energy. Still others claim they come from increasing your frequency or *level of vibrational energy* (that spelled L.O.V.E. in case you missed it, and no I'm not making this up); being returned to the time of birth; or related to breaking through to transpersonal dimensions and otherworldly planes.

Many require adherence to using particular orifices (mouth vs. nose) to breathe through, in a particular order, and for specific periods of time. Many also require the breathing process to be accompanied by specific types of dance, music, bodywork, massage, chants, vocal toning, sound baths, physical exercises and so on for it to be effective.

Most have some sort of pre and post activities to maximize the effects of the process. These can range from simple group discussion and sharing of experiences to the drawing of mandalas and other more esoteric activities.

But I just want to tame my inner asshole.

For the purposes of our journey—managing our inner dialog and taming the inner asshole—we can take a more basic approach. If you want to get involved in an entire package of teachings or a particular philosophy, then go for it. Such choices are a personal matter - whatever tickles your pickle. Find a group that aligns with your interests, beliefs or whatever helps you in your journey!

But I don't want you thinking you have to believe in one approach or version to take advantage of the power of breathwork. Just because some practitioners only sell their brand of healing, and can only explain the effects of breathwork from their exclusive model with all the extras, doesn't make it so.

Any version can work if it's using the underlying principles that drive the necessary change in physiology, creating altered states of mind as a result.

Fast and Intense Breathwork - the essentials

Whether their practitioners are willing to admit it, most types of breathwork rely on similar techniques to achieve their outcomes. At its most basic, this will involve nothing more complicated than lying on the floor, breathing in a circular, connected fashion, faster and deeper than usual.

By using this type of breathing, regardless of the brand of breathwork involved, the underlying principles at work remain roughly the same. An altered or transformational state is achieved because of changes in the concentration of carbon dioxide (CO_2) in the bloodstream, and the amount of oxygen (O_2) available at a cellular level. That's really it, at least from a scientific point of view.

Breathwork, Physiology and Altered States*

Science warning - this section is for those that want an expanded explanation of the physiological processes underpinning fast and intense breathwork. If that's more than you've signed on for, or you're not a science nerd like me, just skip to the next heading, Set and Setting.

Many practitioners, even some of the more famous, will talk about the mind-altering effects of breathwork as resulting from bringing extra oxygen into your body. This is an appealing explanation as it sounds like you're doing something good for yourself, right?

But the effects we're interested in are actually caused by a *decrease* in oxygen (O_2) availability at the cellular level. Specifically, the altered states of consciousness we are seeking to achieve, to reset our inner dialog, are largely a result of too little O_2 reaching the brain.

Somewhat counterintuitively, this decrease in O_2 availability at a cellular level can be caused both by breathing more (deep connected breathing), and by breathing less (breath holds).

It is self-evident why holding your breath—breathing less—would lead to less oxygen being available to your cells. After all, you've stopped breathing . . .

That faster, deeper than usual breathing would also lead to oxygen deprivation at the cellular level needs explanation. It works like this.

Rapid, deep circular breathing has the effect of "blowing off" a larger than usual volume of Carbon Dioxide (CO_2) from the lungs, leading to a lower concentration of CO_2 in the bloodstream. While all this extra breathing simultaneously brings a larger than usual amount of oxygen into the lungs, the amount of O_2 in the bloodstream remains about the same as usual.

The reason for this is quite simple. Oxygen levels in arterial blood normally sit at around 95-98%. So there really isn't any significant capacity for increasing oxygenation in arterial blood leaving the lungs, regardless of how much extra breathing you do. The only significant change at this stage is less CO_2 in the bloodstream.

As CO_2 levels fall, the pH level of the blood is impacted, becoming more alkaline. This effect is known as respiratory alkalosis. Respiratory alkalosis, in turn, impacts how strongly O_2 sticks to the hemoglobin in our red blood cells.

Known as the Bohr Effect, higher alkalinity makes the bond stickier, leading to less O_2 being released to cells around the body—the O_2 stays "stuck" in the red blood cells instead of being handed over to the cells that need it for cellular respiration.

Alkalosis also leads to vasoconstriction, a tightening of small blood vessels that supply the brain, reducing O_2 supply even further. Resulting in the paradoxical situation of inhaling lots of O_2, having high levels of O_2 in our bloodstream, yet at the same time our cells and organs are being starved of oxygen.

In a nutshell, over-breathing leads to the removal of too much carbon dioxide, increasing blood alkalinity, and ultimately causing a cascade of chemical processes that block the passage of oxygen to the cells.

Increased alkalinity also impacts calcium levels within the body, causing neurological effects such as tingling sensations and muscle contractions—including the aforementioned lobster claws, or tetany as it is known medically.

At the same time, larger than normal quantities of endogenous opioids are released within the body, leading to euphoria, and enhanced feelings of physical and mental well-being.

All these chemical processes can explain the range of effects documented during breathwork, including dizziness; tingling in the lips, hands and feet; spasms; muscle cramps; contraction of hands or feet; emotional arousal; disassociation; fight-or-flight responses; and *changes in states of consciousness*.

It is hypothesized that this reduction in oxygen to the brain (up to 40% reduction within one minute of over-breathing exercises), along with the release of various endorphins and endogenous opioids, is responsible for the changes of state reported by breathwork participants.

Some research has specifically identified this reduction in oxygen as being responsible for wreaking havoc on the brain's Default Mode Network or DMN, temporarily reducing "chatter" between its component regions.[5] This network, the "home" of our inner asshole, takes a major hit!

Like a "reboot" of the brain, this interruption of the DMN allows a break from rigid patterns of thought and behavior. The brain, freed of the controls normally imposed by the "bossy" DMN, can enter a state of consciousness less dominated by our inner asshole voices, and more open to new ways of thinking and feeling. While also allowing greater access to unconscious material without the usual sense of judgment.

Just as I had experienced by the end of my session in Amsterdam, it is common for participants to report a feeling of profound calm, a sense of being present, connected, and open.

By deliberately generating a transformational state through breathwork, our normal defenses are downregulated, the usual protective mechanisms of our DMN switched off. We are now more able to load in new information or patterns. And for this reason, it's the perfect time to throw off some of our old negative self-talk, and to focus on alternative stories. A perfect time to give the old asshole a refresh.

Set and Setting. Using Fast Intense Breathwork to retrain our inner assholes.

It's one thing to feel great because we've temporarily altered our state of consciousness, disabling the part of our brain that drives negative self-talk—the Default Mode Network. But that feeling, the 'high', only lasts from a few hours to a few days. We need to have a plan for using this window of opportunity—this transformational state—to change our inner dialog for the long term.

Borrowing from the field of facilitated psychedelic interventions, our plan will revolve around consideration of what has become known as "set and setting."

"Set" refers to someone's mindset at the time of the breathwork experience. This includes beliefs and attitudes, goals for the session, concerns, emotional state, along with anything else that might influence how the person will engage with the experience.

"Setting" is the external environment in which the breathwork experience will be held. Is the environment safe and comfortable? Is there a "sitter" to monitor the breather? Is the session part of a group experience? Is there a facilitator or are they having the experience alone at home? Will there be an opportunity to discuss goals for the session beforehand, and to debrief afterwards?

A well-planned approach to using fast, intense breathwork will take all these questions into account. This ensures the best possible preparation for benefiting from an experience that opens the door to change. By being ready with new affirmations, new scripts, and new strategies to embiggen your mindful self.

Finding a guide

Fast and intense breathwork is, well, *intense*. I believe it should be taken seriously as an intervention and experienced in a facilitated environment—at least until you have some experience with it under your belt. It provides a unique opportunity to enter a transformational state, and is deserving of putting in the requisite pre and post work to really benefit from the experience.

You could do this by engaging a practitioner who provides individual sessions or experience it in a group setting. Online works too. While everyone's needs are different and I cannot be prescriptive, I have found group experiences to be incredibly powerful, especially for first timers.

My advice is to look for practitioners who clearly express an understanding of the application of "set" and "setting" considerations, and who demonstrate some basic appreciation of the science behind the safe use of these practices. Any serious practitioner should take you through a comprehensive explanation of risks, side-effects, and contraindications, and be able to show you a written list of the existing medical conditions that should be considered as risk factors prior to engaging in breathwork.

That said, depending on your proclivities, you may prefer approaches that take a more metaphysical, spiritual, or ceremonial approach to the use of breathwork. Again, whatever floats your boat.

For a down-to-earth but entirely heartfelt approach, I would personally recommend looking at the website BreathwithJP, the online home of John Paul Crimi. I took part in several of his training sessions in LA in early 2020, finding his approach to be a nice balance between sticking with the science, and still providing an incredibly heart-based transformational experience. Or if you're in Europe, look up Sven.*

Regardless of the approach you choose, I think it is instructive to at least be aware of what to expect during a breathwork session. That way, you can make a better-informed decision about what you're getting into and make your choices accordingly.

To that end, I will describe below the fundamental principles that any 'fast and intense' style of breathwork will involve, along with the processes that are at work, regardless of which sacred energy forces are being invoked at the time.

What to expect?

Instructions common to most techniques include:

- Deep diaphragmatic breathing (from deep down in your lower rib cage, rather than higher in your chest).
- Faster than usual breathing. Each deep belly-breath-in is followed by a faster than usual exhale, almost like a quick deep sigh, letting the contents 'fall' out of your lungs.
- Connected breathing. There is no pause between the in and out breath.
- Breath holds. Some techniques will also have you do one or more breath holds in between periods of deep, fast, connected breathing. As the name implies, this simply involves holding your breath for as long as possible.

If you're having trouble visualizing this, there are plenty of examples on the web. Just search for "introduction to breath-work" on YouTube and you'll see lots of demonstrations to give you a clearer picture of what I'm talking about.

By using this type of breathing, regardless of the brand of breathwork involved, the underlying principles at work remain roughly the same. An altered or transformational state is achieved because of changes in the concentration of carbon dioxide in the bloodstream and the amount of oxygen available at a cellular level.

Yet despite its apparent simplicity, breathwork provides a unique window into physiological systems not usually thought of as being under the influence or control of our conscious mind. We can down-regulate our default mode network—silencing the inner asshole—all through readily accessible breathing exercises. We can then use the period of increased receptivity to work on reprogramming our inner dialog, putting our affirmations and visual re-imaging to full effect.

---

*SVEN KIMENAI IS an amazing human being and superb facilitator. Look him up at https://svenkimenai.com/ if you're in Europe seeking a transformational experience involving breathwork and related experiences in nature!

References

1. Zaccaro, A., Piarulli, A., Laurino, M., Garbella, E., Menicucci, D., Neri, B., Gemignani, A. (2018). How Breath-Control Can Change Your Life: A Systematic Review on Psycho-Physiological Correlates of Slow Breathing, *Frontiers in Human Neuroscience,* (12), 353.

2. Noble D. J., Hochman S. (2019). Pulmonary Afferent Activity Patterns During Slow, Deep Breathing Contribute to the Neural Induction of Physiological Relaxation, *Frontiers in Physiology.* (10) 1176

3. Jose L. Herrero, Simon Khuvis, Erin Yeagle, Moran Cerf, & Ashesh D. Mehta. (2018). Breathing above the brain stem: volitional control and attentional modulation in humans. *Journal of Neurophysiology,* 119(1), 145-159.

4. Joan P. Pozuelos, Bethan R. Mead, M. Rosario Rueda, Peter Malinowski (2019). Short-term mindful breath awareness training improves inhibitory control and response monitoring. *Progress in Brain Research,* Vol.244, 137-163.

5. Rhinewine, J. P., & Williams, O. J. (2007). Holotropic breathwork: The potential role of a prolonged, voluntary hyperventilation procedure as an adjunct to psychotherapy. *The Journal of Alternative and Complementary Medicine, 13*(7), 771–776.

6. James Eyerman, J. (2013). A Clinical Report of Holotropic Breathwork in 11,000 Psychiatric Inpatients in a Community Hospital Setting, *Psychedelics in Psychology and Psychiatry,* Spring Vol.23 (1).

18

PUTTING ASSHOLES TO SLEEP

We've all had trouble getting to sleep at times, often because of unwanted, racing thoughts. It feels like the inner asshole is determined to turn sleep-time into prime-time for mindless chatter. Moaning, worrying, and muckraking through every mistake we've ever made and regret we've had.

As we're trying to "downshift" from a busy day, our overactive conscious mind still wants to find things to focus on and "get busy" with. Lacking the stimuli of other people, internet, or TV as we try to fall asleep, it produces its own "entertainment." Unfortunately, the entertainment is often a shit show of unpleasant reruns that stir us up rather than calm us down. These unwanted reruns leave us staring at the ceiling, exhausted but unable to sleep as our minds spool up with ever more distracting stories. So, what can we do?

A number of things actually. We can deliberately choose types of dialog that will occupy our minds and simultaneously help us drift off to sleep. Alternatively, we can run special "movies" of the mind to coax brain activity away from verbal processing networks. And we can also apply techniques that hack our physiology to "switch off" internal dialog.

All these approaches have one thing in common. Making a mindful decision to purposefully choose the show running in our head, rather than leaving it to our mindless inner assholes.

Putting the assholes to sleep.

The default mode network, home of our annoying inner assholes, is activated by the absence of a task to focus our attention on—like when we're lying in bed staring at the ceiling trying to get to sleep. As counterintuitive as it may sound, we need to get active, giving our brain something to do, to relax and switch off the inner asshole. But active in particular ways only. Ones that reduce DMN processing and help the mind and body to relax.

1. Sleep stories and guided meditation.

This option is an increasingly popular and easily accessible method of turning off the inner voices and getting to sleep. Various apps offer sleep stories to distract and lull you into a relaxed state, often with background music and soundscapes designed to enhance the process; guided meditations to relax the body and calm the mind; and various mashups that have elements of both meditation and stories at the same time. You may find yourself simply listening to a story of choice; being instructed on how to breathe; to relax specific muscle groups or parts of the body; or to visualize certain scenes or reflect mindfully on aspects of your life.

A quick Google search for "sleep stories and meditation to get to sleep" will reveal a treasure trove of suggestions, some paid and some free. Experiment and find something that works for you. You were going to be lying there listening to shit-talk from your inner asshole anyway, so what's to lose?

2. *Imagery over words*

This technique taps into two different mechanisms of action at the same time. First, you'll be giving your brain a task that draws activity away from DMN processing regions. Second, you'll also be using a form of mindfulness—drawing attention to the present and away from the rumination of the inner asshole, which focuses more on past regrets and future anxieties.

To use this technique, start by focusing on what you can see with your eyes closed in the dark. Try it now. Close your eyes and just get immensely curious about the myriad patterns, colors, and shapes that you begin to notice. Are there little white specks or lines? Is there movement? Follow the colors, shapes, and movements. Just focus on following them wherever they take you. Stay focused on what these shapes and colors are doing, how they're changing, and where they are going. Are they turning into recognizable objects or people that you know? Just follow wherever these shapes and colors take you.

Do this at night when you want to sleep and notice what happens. Provided you maintain focus on these images, the DMN will be tuned down or deactivated and before you know it, you'll be fast asleep.

3. *Breathing to Sleep*

Our breath matches our physiology. When arousal levels are high—if we're alert and active, with a racing mind or body—

our breath is likely to be more rapid and located in the upper chest. When relaxed, the opposite occurs, with our breath slowing and flowing from the lower abdomen.

Knowing this, we can consciously choose our breathing style, and in doing so, trigger a cascade of physiological changes as our body matches our pace and style of breathing.

By breathing like someone falling asleep, we . . . fall asleep. Slow belly breathing—around 5 or 6 breaths per minute—calm the body and mind, reducing racing thoughts and negativity. Heart rate and blood pressure are reduced, muscles relax, and we increase feelings of peacefulness.

One such technique to quieten the inner asshole is known as the 4-7-8 breathing technique or "relaxing breath." Referred to by one of the world's leaders in integrative medicine, Dr. Andrew Weil, as a "natural tranquilizer for the nervous system," it helps you fall asleep within minutes. For a full description of the technique, review the previous chapter, *Suffocating Assholes*.

4. Self-hypnosis

We're going to dive into the extensive evidence for hypnosis in the next chapter. For now, here are some quick applications of this process for silencing our inner asshole when it comes time to sleep.

There are two main approaches to try. Either using your own internal dialog, or outsourcing the heavy lifting to someone else by listening to one of the many hypnosis tracks and apps available online.

To find online materials, just Google "sleep hypnosis" and "sleep apps." Personal taste plays a big part, so experiment until you find a version you like.

Meantime, if you'd like to go it alone, here's a version of self-hypnosis I've adapted from an old YouTube clip of one of the all-time masters of hypnosis, Milton H. Erickson.

Simply close your eyes, relax your breathing, and slowly and rhythmically count backwards in your mind from 200. As you do, insert the word "sleep" between each count, all the while visualizing, imagining, feeling what the word means. Remembering times when you've been so tired that you couldn't prevent your eyes from closing and falling ... to ... sleep.

So, your internal dialog sounds like this; 200 ... sleep ... 199 ... sleep ... 198 ... sleep ... and so on. Do it slowly in a relaxed internal voice, taking a few seconds to get from one number to the next. In my experience, I have never gotten to 100 before falling fast asleep. The key is to notice if you become distracted and start thinking about something else. And if you do, take yourself back to the task, go back to the beginning (200), and start again. No problem. Nighty night!

5. Switch off inner dialog

There are a few miscellaneous hacks that I've come across over time that can help with turning off the inner asshole. Try them out - I've found them to be incredibly powerful despite their apparent simplicity and ease of use.

a) It's all in the eyes

Just as the way we breathe is aligned to our state of physiological arousal, so too, is our vision. When relaxed, our pupils change, and our vision is expanded. We view the whole environment around us, seeing in "panoramic" vision. Conversely, when our arousal and stress levels are heightened, our vision becomes narrow focused, or tunnel visioned.

And just as we can purposefully change our breathing to reduce our state of physiological arousal and anxiety, so too can we alter our vision to deliberately reduce anxiety and relax the mind when trying to sleep.

This involves expanding our field of vision on purpose. Imagine, for instance, the view from a mountain top, or across an expanse of ocean. There's a reason watching sunsets on a broad expanse of horizon are so relaxing. They require an expanded view, in turn triggering the parasympathetic "rest and digest" nervous system, inducing a state of inner calm.[1]

You can do the same anywhere. Including lying in bed with your eyes closed trying to sleep. Just imagine what it would be like to widen your field of vision, seeing as much as possible without moving your head or eyes. Perhaps imagine yourself on a mountain top soaking in the entire view, eyes unfocused and gazing out to the far horizon.

It takes a little practice, but this technique can put you to sleep in a matter of minutes.

b) Just hold your tongue

In the interest of full transparency, and unlike the rest of the suggestions in this book, I could find little in the way of scientific literature to support this method. With that said, anecdotal evidence and personal experience points to its effectiveness. Given the risk-to-reward ratio—it can't do any harm—why not give it a shot?

So, what's the trick? Well, literally hold your tongue. Yup.

Just as your tongue moves when talking to others, there are also micro-movements associated with internal dialog. By keeping the tongue still, either through relaxing it or holding it in place, we prevent it from "talking" to us.

While some advocates suggest actually grabbing the tongue by the fingers, thankfully there are less nasty ways of achieving the same outcome. You can instead simply press the tip of the tongue behind the teeth and focus on keeping it locked into this position. I find that if I concentrate on pressing it against the back of my front teeth, it becomes surprisingly difficult to maintain any sort of internal dialog.

Alternatively, you can practice completely relaxing the tongue. Simply let it go, imagining it floating loosely in the mouth. Continue to imagine it becoming more and more relaxed, loose, and limp. Focus on nothing else.

c) As a final suggestion, I personally use a mashup of these techniques, with a slight twist. It goes like this.

- With your eyelids closed, let your eyes roll upwards and hold them in this position. According to Neuro-Linguistic Programming (NLP) doctrine, this location is associated with visual processing, and makes the use of internal dialog more difficult.

- At the same time, allow your eyes to flicker slightly from side to side, mimicking patterns of movement found in EMDR therapy and during REM sleep.

- And last, at the same time allow the mouth to fall open slightly while relaxing the tongue.

- Fall asleep. At least, that's what happens to me. Not a pretty sight for anyone I'm sharing the bed with, but what are you going to do . . .

References

1. Warner, J. (2020). Vision and Breathing May be the Secrets to Surviving 2020, *Scientific American*, Nov 16.

19

HYPNOTIZING ASSHOLES

A Hypnotist comes to town

I remember being in my late teens when a famous stage hypnotist was visiting my hometown. Fascinated by the promotion for his show, I bought some tickets and went along with a few friends. I'd never seen anything so bizarre. Audience members, seemingly picked at random, were soon up on stage. Some were clucking like chickens, speaking in unknown languages, or giving birth to various objects. Others were given triggers to react to once they were back in the audience, such as jumping up from their seat and squawking like a frightened bird every time the hypnotist said a certain word.

I wondered if any of this could be real? Were the people on stage some sort of stooges, a part of the act? I was determined to know. I booked in for the next two sessions to be held over coming days, aiming to spot the fakes in the crowd. They had to be a part of his performance, right? It had to be a setup . . .

The History of Hypnosis

The modern day understanding of hypnosis is largely influenced by the Austrian physician Franz Anton Mesmer (1734 - 1815). Mesmer is widely acknowledged as the "Father of Hypnosis," and his surname was the inspiration for an alternative name for the practice still sometimes used today—mesmerism. Mesmer was very much a charismatic showman who used his "mesmerism" in theatrical shows. Such displays were similar to what we would recognize today as stage hypnosis.

In 1843 a Manchester eye doctor and physician, James Braid, renamed mesmerism as "hypnosis." The term refers to Hypnos, the Greek god of sleep. Braid came across hypnosis by chance, noticing one day that a patient was transfixed by the light in his waiting room. He found some people could go into a trance by simply concentrating on the light, or similar bright objects such as a silver watch. Hence the cliched image that many still have today, of people being hypnotized by focusing on a watch or shiny object swinging in front of their eyes.

Jean-Martin Charcot (1825-1893), a leading neurologist of his day, used hypnosis to treat hysteria. Meantime Hippolyte Bernheim (1837-1919), a professor of medicine, described hypnosis as a special form of sleeping, where the subject's attention is focused on the suggestions made by the hypnotist.

The early 19th century saw hypnosis also being used to anesthetize patients during surgery. Scottish surgeon James Esdaile detailed performing 261 painless surgeries in his book *Mesmerism in India, and its Practical Application in Surgery and Medicine.*

With the first generation of anesthetic drugs responsible for killing around 1 in 400 patients, doctors through to the early 20th century continued to use hypnosis either on its own, or in combination with smaller doses of chloroform when performing surgeries. A 1906 report shows the Mayo Clinic had performed over 14,000 operations using hypnosis in this way. Eventually, however, chloroform was replaced by safer compounds and hypnosis fell out of favor as a form of anesthesia.

Despite being replaced by modern anesthetic drugs, it's worth noting researchers have confirmed the historical claim that hypnosis reduces pain for surgical patients. In a 2007 study involving 200 breast cancer patients, those that received a 15-minute pre-surgery hypnosis session reported less post-surgical pain, nausea, fatigue, and discomfort. The study also found that less surgical time was required, along with fewer sedatives and pain-killing drugs during surgery.

The British Medical Association and American Medical Association proclaimed their support for the therapeutic use of hypnosis in medicine in 1955 and 1958, respectively. Today, an International Society of Hypnosis coordinates and assesses standards and practices of professional hypnotists across the world.

A Hypnotist comes to town, Pt.2

Having secured tickets to two more shows, I was certain I was about to crack a case of sure-fire fakery. But it was not to be. None of the audience members who went up on stage to be hypnotized had been in the audience or on stage during previous shows. He seemed to be performing his magic on random audience members. I couldn't work out how he was doing it. I started following people who'd been on stage as they left the performance, asking them about their experience.

To my surprise, all seemed genuine. Some were still confused, unable to explain their own actions; while others had no memory of doing anything strange and would not believe claims that they had clucked like chickens or spoken imaginary foreign languages while on stage. Things just kept getting weirder...

Fast forward twenty years

And so, hypnotism remained a mystery at the back of my mind until about 20 years later. I happened to be watching a popular US talk show when, sure enough, the next guest was a well-known hypnotist. His task? He was about to hypnotize a young woman who had a phobia of spiders.

She explained how she would freeze up and cry violently at the sight of even the tiniest of spiders that she might encounter in daily life. Just talking about it was making her visibly agitated. The hypnotist then did his thing. Under hypnosis, he told her that from now on she would no longer be afraid of spiders. That she would relate to them in the same way that a dog lover would feel about dogs. Brought out of the trance, she said she felt completely relaxed. When asked if she was ready to meet a spider they'd brought along, she nodded excitedly.

What happened next was truly amazing. And a little frightening, even for me watching from the safety of a television screen. From under a small blanket, they revealed a glass cage containing the most hideous spider I'd ever seen - a great fat hairy tarantula as large as a trucker's fist. Removing the glass lid, the spider's handler carefully scooped it up and placed it on the outstretched palm of the woman. Her reaction was priceless. As the spider reared up on its hind legs, appearing to be hissing at the woman, she gently stroked its back with her free hand, all the while cooing, "you're so cute and fluffy . . . who's a little cutie? Yes, you are . . . "

I immediately made a commitment to myself. If this voodoo magic was real, I was going to learn it—ideally from that TV hypnotist! About half an hour of internet research later saw me messaging the hypnotist in question, asking about training with him.

I was excited when I received a message just a few days later, telling me that a part of his practice comprised training for therapists, doctors, and other professionals in related fields. At the time I was enrolled in a Master of Psychology program, and having finished the coursework component of the program, was trying to settle on a thesis topic. I reasoned that the perfect area of research for my thesis would be something related to hypnosis.

The training was incredible. And I was probably a little too enthusiastic by the time I finished. For the next few months, I couldn't help myself. Nobody was safe from my newfound passion. No problem was too big or too small. A friend who couldn't find their keys. Hypnosis was the answer. Out to dinner and someone couldn't decide what they wanted from the menu. Hypnosis. Sister-in-law wanted to stop smoking. You guessed it, hypnosis.

Meanwhile, through my master's program research, I came to realize just how mainstream the practice of hypnosis was in the field of psychology and medicine. A large volume of modern-day research has shown compelling evidence that hypnosis is effective in treating anxiety and stress-related disorders,[4] IBS5, clinical treatment of pain,[6,7] depression,[10,11] and even as the sole anesthetic in various surgical procedures,[8,9] along with myriad other conditions.

So, what exactly is hypnosis?

There is firm evidence for the effectiveness of hypnosis across a wide range of conditions. It is also well supported that, while in a hypnotic state, a person is more susceptible to accepting subconscious suggestions. There is, however, no clear consensus on exactly what it is, or how and why it works.

Many explanations say something like this -

Hypnosis is a state of increased bodily relaxation combined with heightened mental focus and concentration at a subconscious level.

If that sounds a little vague—it does to me—here's my way of explaining it. I define hypnosis *as a way of influencing the unconscious mind directly, bypassing the filters of the conscious mind.*

In this way, hypnosis avoids the usual "checks and balances" carried out by the more logical, conscious mind. Ideas and suggestions land directly in the unconscious without the normal amount of scrutiny, setting up camp amongst all the other ideas and beliefs living in the creaking and overcrowded metropolis of the mind.

From a physiological perspective, the development of fMRI technology has allowed researchers to test what is happening inside the brains of those placed under hypnosis. Such research has demonstrated changes in brain activity. Changes that make sense of the reported experiences of those involved in both clinical and stage hypnosis since it was first popularized over 100 years ago.[1,2] Under hypnosis there is a reduction in activity in the regions of the brain known as the default mode network (DMN)[1,2]—the area responsible for self-focused rumination and reflection—along with greater functional connectivity between the salience network and the executive control network.[1]

These changes would account for the increase in focused attention, enhanced somatic and emotional control, and lack of self-consciousness observed during hypnosis. Meanwhile, evidence of reduced extrinsic lateral frontoparietal cortical connectivity would explain observed decreases in sensory awareness during hypnosis.[3]

The evidence has never been clearer that hypnosis can lead to measurable changes in brain function, behavior, and perceived state of mind. With a demonstrated ability to reduce anxiety and depression, and to enhance states of flow and relaxation, it is an ideal tool for combating our inner assholes.

Hypnosis vs. the inner asshole

One difficulty in dealing with inner assholes is they don't always operate within awareness. Instead, they can whisper their poison in your ear at an unconscious level, staying out of sight as they stoke your fear and anxiety, leaving you to experience a cascade of feelings when facing life's challenges.

You might get nervous, anxious or feel your stomach churning, even though you're not consciously "saying" anything to yourself. Or you might just get an overall sense of dread or fear—often referred to as free floating anxiety—without being able to pin down exactly what's making you feel this way. All a result of sneaky little inner assholes talking you down, behind your back, leaving you to deal with the stinky feelings that bubble up into consciousness as a result.

With hypnosis, however, we can use the same behind-the-scenes processes to tackle these "unconscious assholes." We can set up "automatic" voices that will keep running in the background, beneath our conscious level of awareness. Life-affirming voices that spread the word about how confident, successful, or happy we are. Voices that lead to positive feelings randomly floating into awareness instead.

———

THANKFULLY, it's ridiculously easy these days to try hypnosis. A few years ago, it would have involved an expensive visit to a clinician or therapist who would charge an hourly rate—of course you can still do this if you prefer.

Nowadays, you can try it out in the privacy of your own home. There are hundreds of audio tracks and apps available online, with hypnosis tracks for relaxation, dealing with stress and anxiety, increasing confidence, you name it. And unlike relying on your local therapist, once downloaded, you can use these interventions as often as you like, in whatever setting makes you most comfortable. I recommend listening to such tracks during the hypnagogic state, as you fall asleep at night and after first awaking in the mornings. At such times, the mind becomes especially receptive to being influenced by the hypnotic process.

The at-home approach also neatly addresses the issue of hypnotizability. For those who are most easily hypnotized, a single visit to a clinician might be of great value, since one session can be enough to achieve an immediate result. But if you are less hypnotizable, it might take half a dozen sessions to see a result. That could get expensive.

But with an audio track at home, you can listen every day, twice daily even, until the process kicks in. And from my experience, provided you put in the focus and the time, it *will* kick in, even if it takes a few weeks.

There are so many options to choose from online. I would personally recommend any material from Paul McKenna.

Alternatively, check out the Reveri.com site for a no-nonsense, science-based approach to hypnosis.

Get curious and have some fun with this process. Stick with it for a few weeks if necessary. And expect to see differences in how you think, feel, and act.

References

1. Heidi Jiang, Matthew P. White, Michael D. Greicius, Lynn C. Waelde, David Spiegel, Brain Activity and Functional Connectivity Associated with Hypnosis, *Cerebral Cortex*, Volume 27, Issue 8, August 2017, Pages 4083–4093

2. Deeley Q, Oakley DA, Toone B, Giampietro V, Brammer MJ, Williams SC, Halligan PW. Modulating the default mode network using hypnosis. Int J Clin Exp Hypn. 2012; 60(2):206-28.

3. Demertzi A, Soddu A, Faymonville ME, Bahri MA, Gosseries O, Vanhaudenhuyse A, Phillips C, Maquet P, Noirhomme Q, Luxen A, Laureys S. Hypnotic modulation of resting state fMRI default mode and extrinsic network connectivity. Prog Brain Res. 2011;193:309-22.

4. D Corydon Hammond (2010) Hypnosis in the treatment of anxiety and stress-related disorders, Expert Review of Neurotherapeutics, 10:2, 263-273.

5. William E. Whitehead (2006) Hypnosis for Irritable Bowel Syndrome: *The Empirical Evidence of Therapeutic Effects*, International Journal of Clinical and Experimental Hypnosis, 54:1, 7-20.

6. Jean Holroyd (1996) Hypnosis treatment of clinical pain: Understanding why hypnosis is useful, International Journal of Clinical and Experimental Hypnosis, 44:1, 33-51

7. Chen X, Yuan R, Chen X, Sun M, Lin S, Ye J, Chen C. Hypnosis intervention for the management of pain perception during cataract surgery. *J Pain Res.* 2018;11:1921-1926

8. Facco E. Hypnosis and anesthesia: back to the future. Minerva Anestesiol. 2016 Dec;82(12):1343-1356

20

TRIPPING ASS

"Just say no to drugs." *Nancy Reagan*

"Reality is for the People Who Can't Face Drugs." *Tom Waits*

W hat if you've got a hardcore case of inner asshole voices that just won't shut the f@#k up?

One powerful option for dealing with these assholes is the curated use of psychedelics.

Note I said curated. I'm *not* talking about picking up a pill you found on the ground at a music festival and popping it down your pie-hole. The 5-second rule does not apply. I'm talking about their considered use under thoughtfully constructed circumstances—be they ceremonial, clinical, or other facilitated paradigms.

The use of psychedelics has undergone a significant renaissance over the last 20 years, with a wealth of research indicating their efficacy in dealing with depression, anxiety, and PTSD. In the US, the FDA has granted breakthrough status to such research, fast-tracking trials in the use of psilocybin—the active ingredient of magic mushrooms—as a treatment for major depressive disorder along with MDMA for the treatment of PTSD.

Based on research and evidence to date, such applications of psychedelics also offer promise in dealing a decisive blow to our inner asshole.

A potted history of hallucinogens

Humans have been consuming magic mushrooms and other hallucinogens for thousands of years. They have featured in the spiritual and cultural rituals of peoples across the globe, usually guided by experienced shamans, elders, and other respected members of the cultures in question.

In 1943, Albert Hofmann, a Swiss chemist working for the pharmaceutical company Sandoz, discovered lysergic acid diethylamide's psychoactive nature. You've probably heard of his discovery by its more common name, LSD.

Over the next couple of decades, what followed was a boom in research into the effect of psychoactive compounds. While it may be hard to imagine, given the status of such drugs today, this research was both legal and well supported. Those involved included universities such as Harvard and NYU, professional bodies such as the American Psychiatric Association, and funding from various governments in both the US and Canada. Multiple international conferences, over a thousand clinical papers, and research hubs in the US, Canada, and

Europe studied the effects of these compounds and their possible applications. In the US alone, over a hundred studies were funded by the Federal Government.

Mushrooms themselves became well known in the U.S. through an entirely mainstream source, the iconic American publication, Life magazine. Its May '57 cover story by respected New York banker and amateur mushroom explorer Robert Gordon Wasson describes his mission to southern Mexico to "participate in the age-old rituals of natives who chew strange growths that produce visions."

His story detailing his participation in a mushroom ceremony became a sensation. Yet, it became just one of many articles in Time and Life magazines during the fifties that supported hallucinogenic drugs and their possibilities. Endorsements by professors, businessmen, and celebrities were common, along with positive research reviews, especially regarding their potential for use in conjunction with psychotherapy.

As time passed, psychedelic compounds started to leak out of the research centers and into the general population, becoming particularly popular in the 1960s counterculture movement. To be a hippie was to have tried them. Celebrity icons such as John Lennon, Bob Dylan, Keith Richards, and Mick Jagger traveled to Mexico to experience mushroom ceremonies. At the same time, researchers and psychologists openly discussed their benefits. Keep in mind Johnny Law hadn't stepped in yet, and all this was still relatively uncontroversial, at least through to the late sixties.

Then they became *too* popular. The use of hallucinogens was associated with young people and the anti-war left. None of which made then-President Nixon happy. So, before you know it, Nixon was calling former Harvard psychologist Timothy Leary "the most dangerous man in America" for promoting the widespread use of hallucinogenic drugs. Going on the offensive, Nixon said that people who used drugs were "anti-American" declaring a very public "war on drugs."

By 1970 Congress had enacted the Controlled Substances Act. The Act placed hallucinogenic drugs into Schedule 1, the category reserved for those considered to be most dangerous and with no medical benefit—despite by this time the existence of hundreds of government-funded research papers finding them to be beneficial in treating a range of conditions. As a result, the leading agency providing grants for research on psychedelics, the National Institute of Mental Health (NIMH), stopped funding studies into their therapeutic potential.

And so, this class of drugs that had shown incredible therapeutic promise across thousands of patients—including mushrooms and their active ingredient psilocybin—came to a screaming halt because of a political agenda. Politics, not science, drove the use of mushrooms underground for the next few decades. Meanwhile, the inclusion of psychedelic drugs into Schedule 1 and the prohibition of research into medical applications contributed to the common perception that these drugs are dangerous and addictive.

Magic Mushrooms and Psilocybin

The focus for the rest of this chapter will be on mushrooms and their active ingredient, psilocybin. Psilocybin has been the focus for much of the resurgence in research into the benefits of psychedelics since the nineties. While much of what I am about to explain might also be said for various other hallucinogenic drugs, I will restrict my comments to the active ingredient of magic mushrooms due to this abundance of high-quality research. For those interested, however, growing bodies of research also exist on the highly promising uses for

MDMA, Ketamine, LSD, Ibogaine, and Ayahuasca, to name a few.

Recent research by esteemed medical and educational institutions such as Johns Hopkins University—and published in highly regarded scientific journals such as JAMA Psychiatry—has shown that psilocybin-assisted therapy produces large, rapid, and sustained antidepressant effects in patients with major depressive disorder.[1]

Meanwhile, in a head-to-head comparison of psilocybin with a typical antidepressant medication—escitalopram—researchers at Imperial College London found symptom remission rates were twice as high in the psilocybin group as the escitalopram group.[2]

Small studies of psilocybin-assisted therapy have also suggested positive results in treating alcohol and nicotine addictions. Meanwhile, fMRI studies have demonstrated that psilocybin impacts the activity of that source of unwanted inner dialog, the brain's default mode network.[3,4]

Keep in mind participants in these sorts of trials undergo at most only a few sessions using psilocybin, yet report lasting effects as a result. Unlike traditional antidepressants that only work for as long as they are taken, participants report fundamental changes in how they see and feel about themselves and the world around them. Experiences that change their ongoing relationship with their inner voices.

How does this work? What are psychedelics doing to the brain to help reduce anxiety and depression, and to fight our inner asshole?

The Default Mode Network (DMN)

The default mode network, or DMN for short, is the name given to a network of brain regions associated with thinking about ourselves. Remembering the past and imagining the future. It primarily focuses on our role in these memories and future scenarios. How we did, what others might think of us, and what might become of us. Plus, it's a worrier. It's these regions that generate our scared, anxious voices. The ones that pick over all our problems and faults, jumping from one issue to the next in a never-ending cycle of blame, shame, and fear. It's most active when our brain is in "idle" mode, firing up when we're not busy with specific activities or tasks. For instance, when we're mindlessly staring at a computer screen or television. Perhaps lying in bed trying to get to sleep. Or attempting to relax, meditate, and otherwise de-stress.

Not surprisingly, given its role in worrying and excessive rumination, research has shown the DMN is associated with conditions such as depression, anxiety, and schizophrenia. When overactive, it can turn healthy self-reflection into faulty and unnecessarily negative self-criticism.

Knowing how to turn off or tune out the DMN sits at the root of many, if not all, traditional and modern concepts of calming and reclaiming peace of mind.

Psilocybin, the active hallucinogenic ingredient in magic mushrooms, significantly impacts the operation of the DMN.[5] Under the influence of psilocybin, connections between regions of the brain that make up the DMN effectively "dissolve," leaving your brain free to operate without the usual constraints imposed by your inner dialog.

This rapid disintegration of the DMN's control is thought to be associated with the feelings of ego-dissolution that people usually report after taking a psychedelic substance. As the grip of our usual sense of self falls away, so too does a sense of the boundaries typically experienced between ourselves and the world around us. All the things that make us different, separate us, hold us back and lock us into our way of thinking and being, collapse in on themselves. We experience what it feels like to be without rules, without rumination, without an unforgiving inner voice.[5,6]

Set and Setting

Following a psychedelic experience, we have a unique window of opportunity to play a part in how the DMN puts itself back together. Our brain, tipped into a transformational state by psychedelic medicine, is open to new interpretations, new rules.[6]

To maximize this receptive state, we must be prepared for the opportunity to guide the rewiring of our brains. This is why the random use of psychedelics at your local festival is not going to achieve the same results being discussed here. The carefully curated mindset with which these powerful plant medicines are approached, along with the environment in which they are used, is critical to the outcome of any deliberate intervention. This means addressing what has come to be known as *set and setting*.

Set refers to someone's mindset at the time of the psychedelic experience. This includes beliefs and attitudes, goals for the session, related experiences, concerns about the upcoming treatment, and anything else that might influence how the person will engage with the experience.

Setting is the external environment in which the experience will be held. Is the environment safe and comfortable? Is there a facilitator, or are you having the experience alone at home? Will there be an opportunity to discuss goals for the experience beforehand and to debrief afterward? What is the integration process for linking the psychedelic experience with ongoing life experience? Have you come to the experience armed with a clear set of affirmations and new images, to be used in your affirmation and visualization process as your DMN puts itself back together?

So, if you're thinking, hey, I've tried psychedelics at a party once, and I'm still a hot mess of inner asshole voices, this could be the reason why. Unless the use of such powerful agents is carefully curated, they may provide nothing more than a bizarre experience in the moment.

Planning for change

A solid plan for making use of the window of change created by psychedelics involves three considerations -

- Preparation (what do we need to consider before the session?)
- The Experience (how will we conduct the actual psychedelic experience?)
- Integration (how will we integrate the experience to change our inner story?)

It doesn't need to be a complex plan. It might be as simple as deciding on a particular question or goal for the experience. And then spending a few days leading up to the experience reflecting or meditating on that specific outcome. The idea is that we're setting a focus for our unconscious mind, one that will hopefully set a direction for the experience itself.

During the psychedelic ceremony or session, one would reaffirm the area in which guidance is being sought. But also, be open to whatever the unconscious then produces and provides. It's a little like white water rafting. We may have a destination in mind but can't dictate how and where the rapids might throw us around during the journey. But setting a goal at least "directionalizes" the process, and we're more likely to end up somewhere useful.

Coming out of the process, it is useful to spend time reflecting on the experience. One might sense a clear answer to the question they went in with. Other times, a clear answer to something better may arise. Regardless of such specifics, inner assholes are more subdued following the psychedelic experience, leaving participants open to the new. The *mindful self* is back in charge, at least for a while. And with ego barriers having been knocked aside, there is a unique opportunity to participate mindfully in their reconstruction as ego boundaries slowly rebuild over the coming days.

This time of integration can be spent focusing on new "rules" to live one's life by, to sneak in some new self-talk patterns. It is a perfect time to work on all aspects of self, focusing on positive affirmations, love and kindness meditation, and reflection. Deliberately looking for the positive in people and situations. Knowing that doing so during this period of high brain plasticity helps to rebuild our inner voices as coaches, not assholes.

Experiencing Psychedelics

I cannot, of course, speak to the legality of the practices we've been reviewing in your particular jurisdiction, or recommend specific guides or therapists in your location. Such information is continually evolving, with, for instance, several jurisdictions in the U.S. decriminalizing the use of psilocybin over recent years. I can, however, suggest a range of options for learning more about this strategy when dealing with your inner assholes.

There are many psychedelic societies and information groups around the world. There are also numerous legal psychedelic retreats held regularly in different locations globally. Any legal and legitimate providers of such experiences will guide you through associated health considerations and contraindications—don't get involved if such issues are not being fully addressed.

A great starting point for information is the Multidisciplinary Association for Psychedelic Studies—MAPS—website. At the same time, Michael Pollan's book *How to Change Your Mind* provides an excellent primer on all things psychedelic. For a good feel of how a professionally run experience blending science and ceremony operates, check out Synthesis Retreats, based in Amsterdam. For yet more information, try this link for a global list of psychedelic societies, or Google "Psychedelic Society - Airtable."

References

1. Davis AK, Barrett FS, May DG, et al. Effects of Psilocybin-Assisted Therapy on Major Depressive Disorder: A Randomized Clinical Trial. *JAMA Psychiatry.* 2021;78(5):481–489.

2.   https://www.reuters.com/world/uk/magic-mushroom-compound-least-good-antidepressant-uk-study-2021-04-14/

3. Bogenschutz MP, Forcehimes AA, Pommy JA, Wilcox CE, Barbosa PC, Strassman RJ. Psilocybin-assisted treatment for

alcohol dependence: a proof-of-concept study. J Psychopharmacol. 2015 Mar;29(3):289-99.

4. Johnson, M. W., Garcia-Romeu, A., & Griffiths, R. R. (2017). Long-term follow-up of psilocybin-facilitated smoking cessation. *The American journal of drug and alcohol abuse, 43*(1), 55–60.

5. Barrett, F.S, Krimmel, S.R., Griffiths, R.R., Seminowicz, D.A., Mathur, B.N. (2020). Psilocybin acutely alters the functional connectivity of the claustrum with brain networks that support perception, memory, and attention, *NeuroImage*, Volume 218.

6. Carhart-Harris, R.L., Roseman, L., Bolstridge, M. *et al.* Psilocybin for treatment-resistant depression: fMRI-measured brain mechanisms. *Sci Rep* 7, 13187 (2017)

7. Roseman, L., Leech, R., Feilding, A., Nutt, D. J., & Carhart-Harris, R. L. (2014). The effects of psilocybin and MDMA on between-network resting state functional connectivity in healthy volunteers. *Frontiers in human neuroscience, 8*, 204.

21

FLOW, MINDFULNESS AND A LIFE WELL LIVED...

Finding Flow

E ven though it was 20 years ago, I remember it like yesterday. I had decided to hire a Jujitsu master to train me personally a couple of times per week in the finer arts of self-defense.

For some reason, during one particular class, he was highlighting the value of knowing how to defend myself from a long-handled ax attack. Now, I'm not sure how often people are attacked by aggressors swinging axes with 5-foot handles. Still, he seemed to think it was an important thing to prepare for. And I didn't feel in a position to be arguing with him as he demonstrated various ways that someone might try to chop me into tiny pieces.

Then he said it was time to practice. Actual gulp. He explained he would gradually move towards me, swinging the ax in a wide figure-of-eight pattern as he advanced.

My job was to stay out of range of the swings while simultaneously studying the timing of his movements. At the appropriate
time, while the ax was at the lowest point of its arc and immediately before it had begun to rise again for the next swing, I was
to *step forward into* the striking range of the ax. To flow with the
motion of the ax handle using its own momentum as I blocked
and parried. Hmm. Sure, buddy.

In fairness to all those caring readers concerned on my behalf
as they read this, the ax head itself was covered in a rubberized
sheath for practice purposes. However, it would still hurt—a lot
—if I was hit in full swing. Especially if I timed it wrong, and it
came down on my head.

My instructor called out, "are you ready?" and started swinging
at me, seeming to mistake my disbelieving silence with consent.
What happened next is the part I've never forgotten since. My
mental state magically transformed. I found myself entirely in
the "now," a pure presence of mind that felt immensely
peaceful and calming. All concerns about the future, misgiv-
ings over the past—including my decision to take Jujitsu
lessons—were gone. I was totally present and at one with my
surroundings.

I was enjoying what is sometimes called a *flow state*, the experience of being completely "in the zone." Like a scene from the
Matrix, I felt as if time had slowed down, that I had somehow
stepped out of my body, able to observe both the flow of the ax
and my own movements dispassionately, all in slow motion.

I had accidentally discovered the experience of *flow* for myself
—what it feels like when the brain regions responsible for
generating our inner asshole dialog are silenced.

Flow and the Default Mode Network

The flow state is often reported by people who are totally immersed in some task or activity. A sense of being wholly absorbed by what they are doing, and as a result losing all sense of time; enjoying a feeling of being outside of everyday reality; all often accompanied by an unusually heightened sense of serenity. A sense of having stepped outside of one's usual worries or concerns, feeling so engrossed in the experience that other needs become insignificant.

It is perhaps not surprising that having a long-handled ax swinging at my head would have the effect of sharpening my focus of attention. The surprising part, however, was this amazing feeling of flow, not fear. Which makes sense in retrospect. There was no time for fear.

Instead, I found complete and absolute inner peace, with all my many inner asshole voices coming to a full stop as I focused on avoiding the swinging ax. It was serene.

This fits perfectly with what we know about the Default Mode Network. After all, if the DMN, the home of our annoying inner assholes, is activated by the absence of a task to focus our attention on—like when we're lying in bed staring at the ceiling trying to get to sleep—imagine the opposite effect. The act of having to avoid the ax had dialed up my focus to an 11 out of 10, completely overriding the grip of the inner asshole.

Working out the timing of when to jump *towards* a swinging ax requires 100% focus and attention. There's no time for a bit of by-the-way idle chit-chat from some inner asshole about why Mary in accounting gave me a sideways look last week. The DMN is dialed right back, along with all the voices that usually emanate from these regions of the brain.

So how do we turn off our inner assholes, dial down the DMN and feel the relaxation of flow without an ax being swung at our head?

How do we make *flow* a part of our everyday experience? And in so doing, live a life free of the inner asshole.

Good question, grasshopper . . .

Reaching Flow

There are lots of ways to reach flow. No doubt you've experienced some of them—becoming so fully immersed in a process or activity, so engrossed that time passes by without notice, and the concerns of everyday life are forgotten.

It could be playing sports or engaging in hobbies, feeling almost "at one" with the bat, racket, or ball. Play becomes virtually unconscious as you instinctively move through the game.

The same can be felt during dancing, cycling, or running. Or during pursuits like painting, drawing, reading, writing, or playing video games. Or losing yourself down the rabbit hole of social media posts, Instagram images, and Tik Tok videos. You become fully immersed in the activity with hunger, thirst, fatigue, or boredom wholly forgotten.

Doing a job you love can deliver the same experience, making sense of the aphorism that finding a job you love and making it your vocation means you'll never have to work another day of your life.

Our experience of life during a flow state is an excellent example of what becomes possible when we turn off, dial back, or otherwise interrupt the patterns of our DMN, along with the unwanted chatter of our inner assholes.

Imagine being able to step into such a state whenever you want. To be able to turn off the nagging voices that make you sick, anxious, or depressed. To transition from negative patterns of thought, finding inner calm, stillness, and relaxation.

Experiencing a life of inner calm is possible, and these flow states give us a taste of what it might be like to live inside a quieter mind, one that is not regularly bombarding you with their never-ending stories.

Finding flow through mindfulness

Flow experiences result from complete connection with life in any given moment, providing states of peak enjoyment, energetic focus, and peace of mind.[1]

This state of enjoyment away from the nagging of the inner asshole can also be cultivated through the practice of mindfulness—deliberately maintaining moment-to-moment awareness of your thoughts, feelings, and your immediate environment. The more you practice being mindful, the better your mind becomes at paying attention to whatever you choose to focus on. This trains your brain to become better at slipping into flow; complete absorption in whatever you turn your attention to. Be it your favorite sport, your work, or a conversation with a loved one.

Various religious and spiritual practices have long-taught followers to calm their inner voices through exercises that dampen the DMN and develop a sense of flow—often using mindfulness meditation and similar practices. While different practitioners and practices vary their emphasis on particular aspects of mindfulness, it can be defined as -

Focusing on whatever is happening, being fully present with whatever you're sensing or feeling in the moment, without interpretation or judgment. Witnessing and noticing each present moment compassionately, yet without connecting or becoming attached to it. Recognizing that thoughts are merely thoughts, rather than suppressing or clinging to them, one simply observes them as passing events...

We cannot control the thoughts, memories, or images that may come our way, but mindfulness is the practice of choosing to attend *or not* to those thoughts. Learning to let each thought or image simply float past like clouds in the sky, rather than fixate on them as they appear.

This approach can be practiced anytime. Take, for instance, an everyday conversation with a friend or work colleague. This is no less an opportunity for practicing mindfulness and experiencing flow.

Imagine being truly *present* during this or any conversation. To truly listen mindfully, stop doing or thinking about anything else—including judging what they are saying or preparing your response—to just breathe naturally, listen to every word said, and sense their emotion, all without an agenda. To get curious. To become genuinely fascinated and absorbed in *their* experience. And then to be capable of reflecting to them the essence of what they have said, better than they could express it themselves.

Imagine for a moment what a conversation like that might do for any relationship. To truly be present for another person without judgment and to leave them feeling fully listened to, truly understood...

Yes, opportunities for mindfulness, to cultivate flow experiences where we allow ourselves to become fully absorbed in the life around us, present themselves constantly.

Mindfulness and the Inner Asshole

A mindfulness approach to dealing with the inner assholes is one of acceptance. Instead of being baited by them or trying to resist them, we simply accept them, letting them drift past like clouds in an otherwise clear blue sky.

We focus on practicing nonjudgmental awareness of our present moment, especially our thoughts, feelings, and bodily sensations. We notice our inner dialog with detached curiosity, openness, and curiosity, without making it stronger by focusing on it and fighting it. We don't give it oxygen in the form of the attention it craves, but instead, as Buddha said, we just *let that shit go . . .*

Ok, I made that last quote up, but I'm sure Buddha would agree with the sentiment.

We maintain absolute focus on our present moment, not on the commentary of our inner assholes. If our thoughts wander—if we find ourselves starting to identify with a particular internal dialog—we simply bring our attention back to the moment. How our body feels, our breathing, or the detail of whatever is happening around us. The task we're performing or the person we're talking to.

This may sound a bit wishy-washy, but research shows that cultivating our *mindful self* is a highly effective way of taming the inner asshole.

A Sampling of the Evidence

Here is a small selection of headline findings from respected peer-reviewed medical and scientific journals, researching the impact of mindfulness practices on mental health and wellbeing. Just Google the article names provided if you feel like checking out the full details.

From "Mindfulness-based interventions for psychiatric disorders: A systematic review and meta-analysis," in the Clinical Psychology Review, 2018.

• A review of over 12,000 participants in 142 non-overlapping samples to determine the efficacy of mindfulness based interventions for a wide range of disorders including depression, anxiety, phobias, and PTSD.

• The meta-analysis showed mindfulness therapies to be overall superior to no treatment, while matching or exceeding active control interventions (i.e., control groups using the psychological treatments).

• On average, mindfulness practices were equivalent to first-line evidence-based therapies and antidepressant medications.

From "Efficacy of Mindfulness-Based Cognitive Therapy in Prevention of Depressive Relapse: An Individual Patient Data Meta-analysis From Randomized Trials," published by the American Medical Association in JAMA Psychiatry, 2016.

• A study of 1258 patients showed a reduced risk of depressive relapse.

• Mindfulness-based cognitive therapy showed efficacy in treating relapse prevention of those with recurrent depression.

• Efficacy was even more pronounced for those with more severe symptoms prior to treatment.

FROM "EFFECTS of Mindfulness on Psychological Health: A Review of Empirical Studies," in the Clinical Child and Family Psychology Review, 2011.

• Found that mindfulness induces a variety of positive psychological effects.

• Improved wellbeing.

• Reduced emotional reactivity.

• Improved self-regulation of behavior.

FROM "THE BENEFITS of being present: mindfulness and its role in psychological wellbeing" published by the American Psychological Association in the Journal of Personality and Social Psychology, 2003.

• Found that mindfulness is associated with enhanced self-awareness.

• Mindfulness predicts the use of self-regulated behavior and maintenance of positive emotional states.

• A clinical study with cancer patients demonstrated increases in mindfulness related to a reduction in mood disturbance and stress.

FROM "EFFECTIVENESS and cost-effectiveness of mindfulness-based cognitive therapy compared with maintenance antidepressant treatment in the prevention of depressive relapse or recurrence (PREVENT): a randomised controlled trial," in The Lancet, 2015.

•424 patients with three or more previous major depressive episodes were randomly assigned to either maintenance anti-depressants or Mindfulness-based cognitive therapy (MBCT).

•Primary outcome of the study was relapse or recurrence of depression.

•MBCT was equivalent to maintenance antidepressants in preventing relapse over the 24 months trial.

THE ABILITY TO keep your mind focused on the present—rather than ruminating about the past and worrying about the future —is strongly correlated with greater psychological well-being.[2] The more you can choose a mindful state in the face of life's ups and downs, the less suffering you will experience.[3]

Practicing Mindfulness and finding Flow

Mindfulness is about giving yourself totally to the present, to whatever is happening in front of you. There are so many ways to practice such a mindset.

Try some of these:

- Focus on your breathing. Take time out throughout the day to observe how you're breathing. Notice the qualities of your breath. Are you breathing shallow into your chest or deep into your belly? How fast are you breathing? Try slowing it down for a few minutes, around 5-6 breaths per minute.
- Read something that interests you. Let yourself get lost in the experience.
- Eat mindfully. Every bite should be a joy. Consciously chew longer, noticing the flavors.

- Walk. Walking really does clear your head and leave you feeling better.[5] And if you can, take a walk in nature. Research has shown a 90-minute walk in a natural setting experienced reduced levels of negative internal dialog and reduces activity in an area of the brain linked to risk for mental illness.[4]
- Find something creative to do. Engaging in creative endeavors that you enjoy is one of the most sure-fire ways to get into a flow state. It could be anything from painting, pottery, cooking, doodling, singing, gardening, knitting—you name it.
- Help someone, anyone. Focusing on the needs of others reduces damaging inner dialog, stress, and depression. Plus, it feels good! Start with doing someone a small favor. Every bit counts!
- Listen to some music. Play something that really engages you and let yourself be immersed in the sound.
- Find something to laugh about. Laughing is the ultimate in-the-moment activity. Find the humor in the little things in life. There's a lot of funny shit going on when you really think about it.
- Create a journal. There's a ton of research showing that writing a journal helps clarify and put negative thoughts into perspective and helps reduce anxiety and depression. [6,7]
- Exercise.
- Mindfulness meditation. Sit and experience your entire body. Really notice each feeling and sensation. Use one of the many guided mindfulness meditation apps available if you like.
- Stop and notice how much there is to be grateful for in any given moment.
- Practice random acts of kindness.

- Take a hot bath. Try a sauna or floatation tank. Just soak in the experience of something different going on for your body. Relax.
- Really focus on those around you, looking for reasons for a genuine compliment.
- Listen. Really listen to someone when they are talking. Listen for what they are saying and what they are not saying. Listen for the emotion behind their words. Don't interrupt; don't judge, and don't be distracted by your own internal dialog. Just listen.

The best revenge on your inner asshole is a life well-lived . . .

The more you get out of your head and into the moment, the more life you will live. Because life is what's in front of you right now. There is only the present. The past is the past, and the future does not exist. Just a series of endless "nows"—the eternal present.

Following the endless chatter of the inner assholes constantly takes you down the rabbit hole and through the looking glass into imagined worlds. If those worlds are full of demons from the past and flying monkeys whipping you into a frenzy about what might go wrong in the future, then it's time to change where you spend your time.

Get your head out of your ass and into the now. Be present. Be mindful. Now is where the action is.

Go get some.

References

1. Csikszentmihalyi, M. (2000). *Beyond boredom and anxiety.* Jossey-Bass.

2. Brown, K.W, Ryan, R.M. The benefits of being present: Mindfulness and its role in psychological well-being. *J Pers Soc Psychol.* 2003;84(4):822–848.

3. Bodhi, B. What does mindfulness really mean?: A canonical perspective. *Contemporary Buddhism.* 2011;12(1):19–39.

4. Gregory N. Bratman, J. Paul Hamilton, Kevin S. Hahn, Gretchen C. Daily, James J. Gross (2015). Nature reduces rumination and sgPFC activation, *Proceedings of the National Academy of Sciences.* 112 (28) 8567-8572.

5. Miller JC, Krizan Z. (2016). Walking facilitates positive affect (even when expecting the opposite). *Emotion.* Aug;16(5):775-85.

6. Mercer, A., Warson, E., Zhao, J. (2010). Visual journaling: An intervention to influence stress, anxiety and affect levels in medical students, *The Arts in Psychotherapy,*Vol. 37, (2), 143-148.

7. Stice E, Burton E, Bearman SK, Rohde P. (2007) Randomized trial of a brief depression prevention program: an elusive search for a psychosocial placebo control condition. *Behav Res Ther.* 45(5):863-76

ACKNOWLEDGMENTS

It's been a long time between drinks. My first book, *Skroo The Rules - What the worlds most productive workplace does differently,* was published just over 20 years ago. A lot of people, for a long time, have put up with me telling them there would be another book coming.

Having finally caught up with my promises, I'd like to acknowledge the support and encouragement of some of the people who've helped me stay on track. Chloe Cobbin, my editor, challenged me in our very first meeting when she asked me what my goal was for the book. Did I want it to be good, or did I want it to be great? Her simple question put me on the spot, and made me realize that I wanted to step up my ambitions for the project. Her ensuing efforts in shaping the work were invaluable, both in terms of her creative input and her proofing and editing skills. Also, in terms of creative inputs, I'd like to give a special thanks to the amazing Laura Roberts who worked on several iterations of book cover design.

Thanks too, to the array of friends and colleagues who put up with, and provided feedback, on my never-ending ramblings about the book and its content, many of whom also took the time to read parts of the manuscript, provide feedback and make suggestions. Such stars include my daughter Lily, my friends Jenny T., Scott W., Keith S., Marcus S., Paul M., Glenn R., Jade and Josh O., Rob D., Zoe M., Maya P., my neighbor and fellow writer Amber M., and the amazing crews at my local coffee shops—where I spent many hours typing—Uncommon Ground, West End Coffee House, and Blackstar.

Finally, thank-you to all the random friends, seminar participants, colleagues and complete strangers who supported the concept of this book—immediately identifying with its title, and in the process constantly refreshing my motivation to finish the book. A motivation to produce something that resonated with—and would hopefully help—those who, like me, have a voice in their head that's an asshole.

ABOUT THE AUTHOR

Hi I'm Darryl Blake, M.Psych., author, educator and all round asshole-whisperer.

I speak and write about psychology and self-development, breaking down complex concepts and jargon into accessible, evidence-based tools for change.

Over the last 20 years I have helped individuals and companies develop and grow, with over 25,000 participants attending my seminars across North America, the UK and AsiaPacific.

For more information about my next book, and how to get involved with the 'Way of the Whisperer Retreat', a legal psychedelic assisted change program held in Jamaica and Amsterdam, visit voiceheadasshole.com

Made in the USA
Middletown, DE
05 June 2022

66700476R00139